STAY AT HOME
SCARFACE

KENNY KEIL

THE DEVASTATOR

WRITTEN & DRAWN BY
KENNY KEIL

EDITORS
GEOFFREY GOLDEN & AMANDA MEADOWS

ISBN-10: 1-942099-09-6

ISBN-13: 978-1-942099-09-3

First Edition: May 2016

devastatorpress.com

PRINTED IN ~~CUBA~~ KOREA

SAY HELLO
TO MY LiTTLE
BOOK.

PROLOGUE

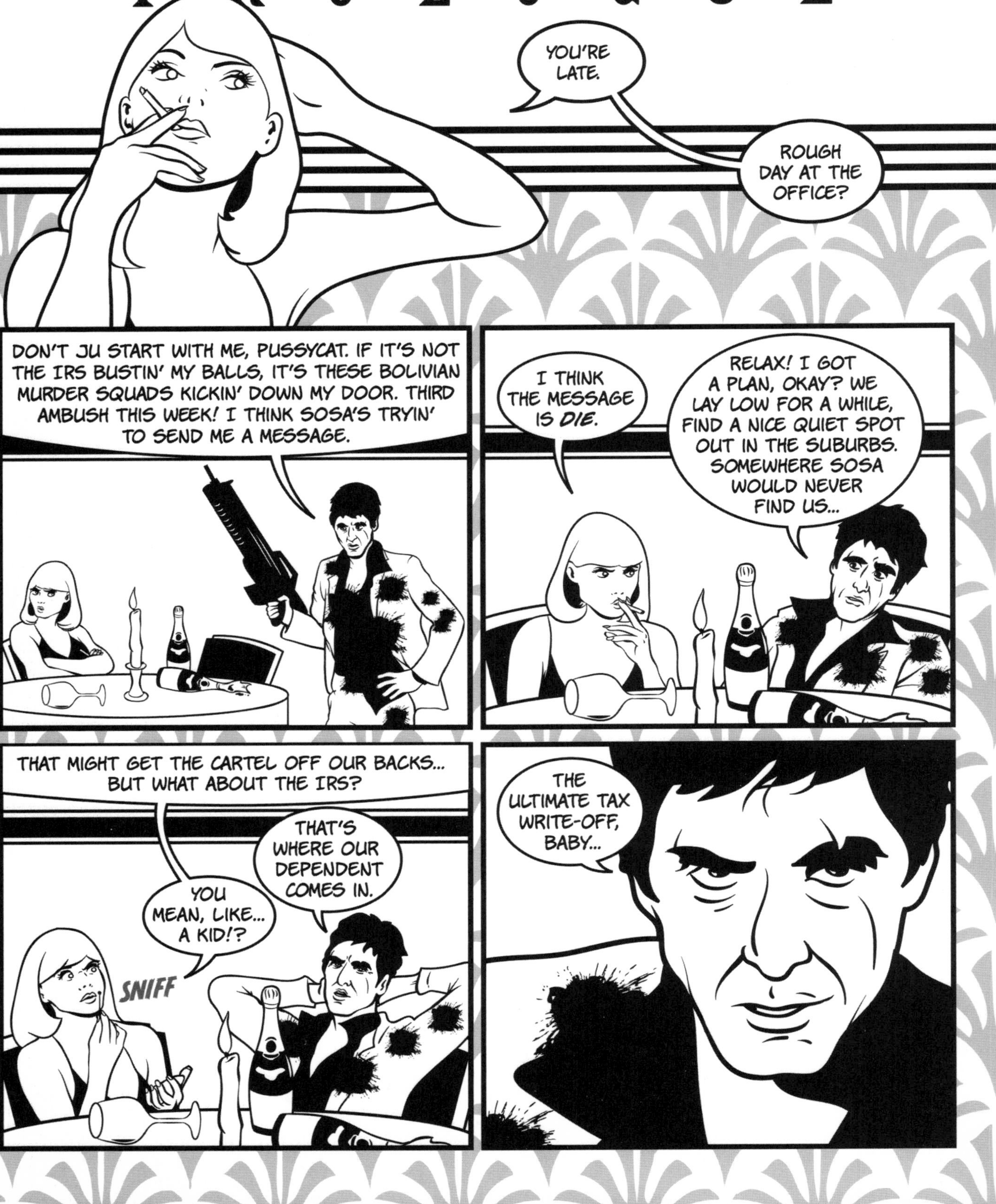

YOU'RE LATE.
ROUGH DAY AT THE OFFICE?
DON'T JU START WITH ME, PUSSYCAT. IF IT'S NOT THE IRS BUSTIN' MY BALLS, IT'S THESE BOLIVIAN MURDER SQUADS KICKIN' DOWN MY DOOR. THIRD AMBUSH THIS WEEK! I THINK SOSA'S TRYIN' TO SEND ME A MESSAGE.
I THINK THE MESSAGE IS *DIE*.
RELAX! I GOT A PLAN, OKAY? WE LAY LOW FOR A WHILE, FIND A NICE QUIET SPOT OUT IN THE SUBURBS. SOMEWHERE SOSA WOULD NEVER FIND US...
THAT MIGHT GET THE CARTEL OFF OUR BACKS... BUT WHAT ABOUT THE IRS?
THAT'S WHERE OUR DEPENDENT COMES IN.
YOU MEAN, LIKE... A KID!?
SNIFF
THE ULTIMATE TAX WRITE-OFF, BABY...

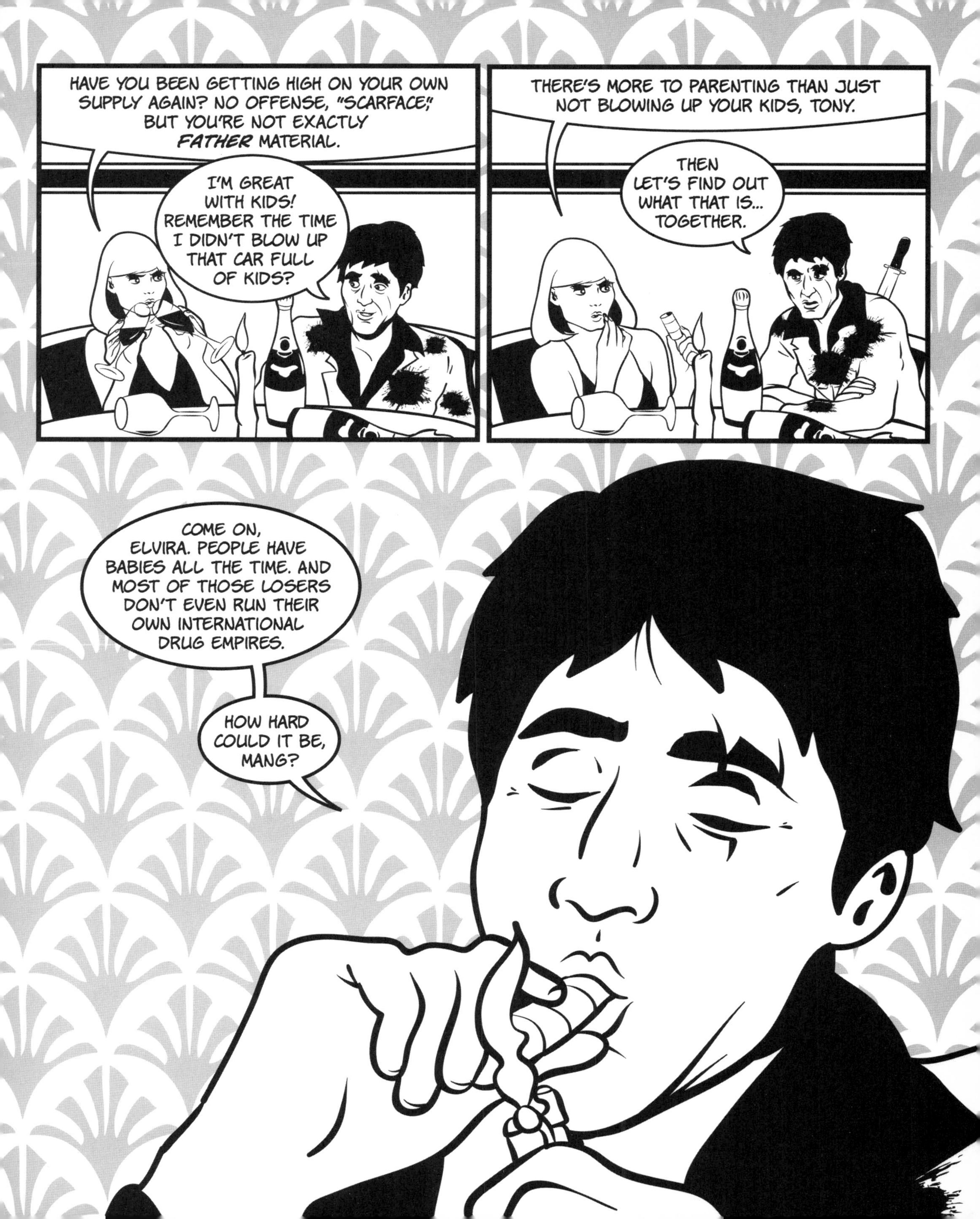
HAVE YOU BEEN GETTING HIGH ON YOUR OWN SUPPLY AGAIN? NO OFFENSE, "SCARFACE," BUT YOU'RE NOT EXACTLY *FATHER* MATERIAL.
I'M GREAT WITH KIDS! REMEMBER THE TIME I DIDN'T BLOW UP THAT CAR FULL OF KIDS?
THERE'S MORE TO PARENTING THAN JUST NOT BLOWING UP YOUR KIDS, TONY.
THEN LET'S FIND OUT WHAT THAT IS... TOGETHER.
COME ON, ELVIRA. PEOPLE HAVE BABIES ALL THE TIME. AND MOST OF THOSE LOSERS DON'T EVEN RUN THEIR OWN INTERNATIONAL DRUG EMPIRES.
HOW HARD COULD IT BE, MANG?

GET A WOMB

Whoa! It really *is* polluted in here! How am I gonna find my way through this mess?

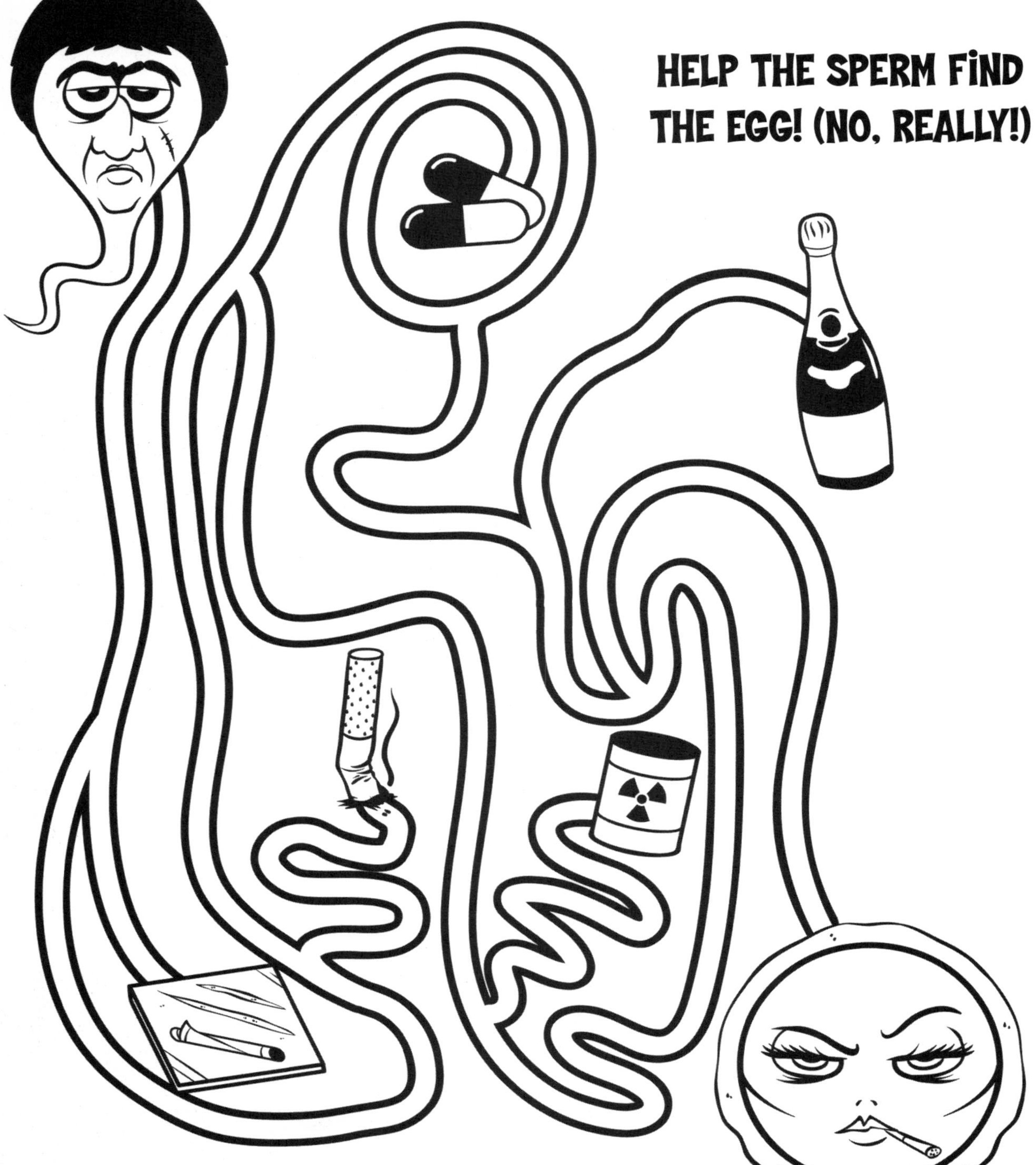
HELP THE SPERM FIND THE EGG! (NO, REALLY!)

NINE MONTHS LATER...

TONY PiCKS A NAME

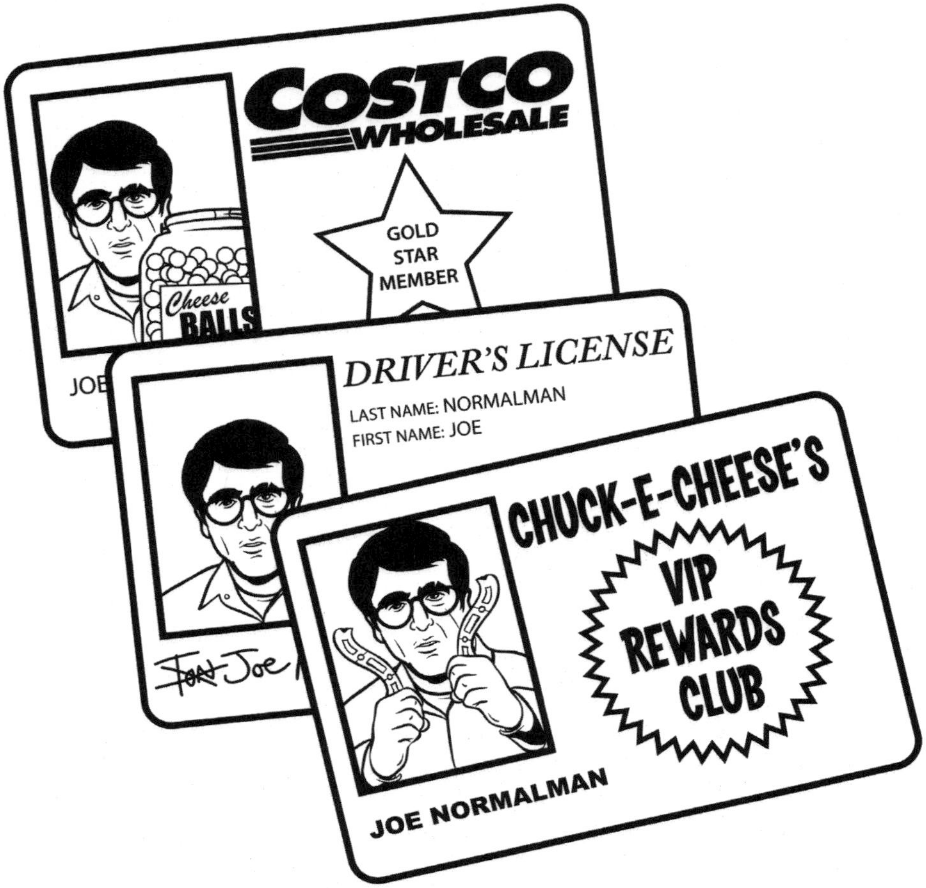

COSTCO
WHOLESALE
GOLD STAR MEMBER
Cheese BALLS
JOE
DRIVER'S LICENSE
LAST NAME: NORMALMAN
FIRST NAME: JOE
CHUCK-E-CHEESE'S
VIP REWARDS CLUB
JOE NORMALMAN

Ju think running a drug empire is hard?
Try having a baby, mang. I got responsibilties comin' out my culo!

The kid is due any day now. Elvira says I need to hurry up and pick a name. So I yell back, "TONY MONTANA DON'T TAKE ORDERS FROM NOBODY" until I forget what I was yelling about – – and then suddenly I realize, I need to hurry up and pick a name! It's kind of a crucial step if ju gonna assume a fake identity.

So, say goodnight to the bad guy...
and say hello to "Joe Normalman!"

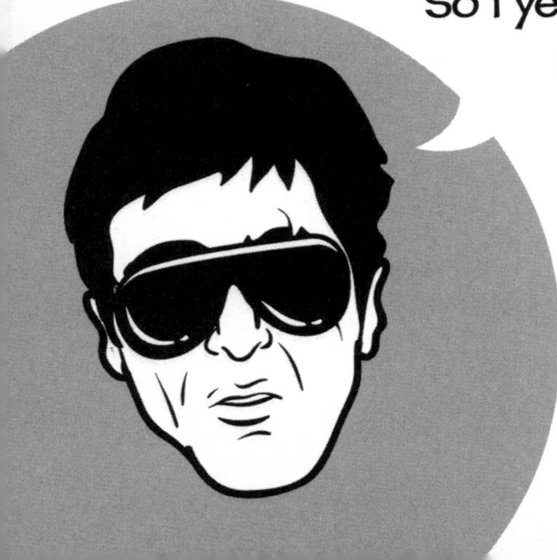

AND ONE FOR THE BABY, TOO

So it turns out Elvira meant I needed to pick a name *for the baby*.
Are ju thinking what I'm thinking?

NOMEY

SERCETP

PWERO

AINCCEO

**SOLVE THE WORD JUMBLE TO NAME THE BABY.
IT AIN'T ROCKET SCIENCE, MANG.**

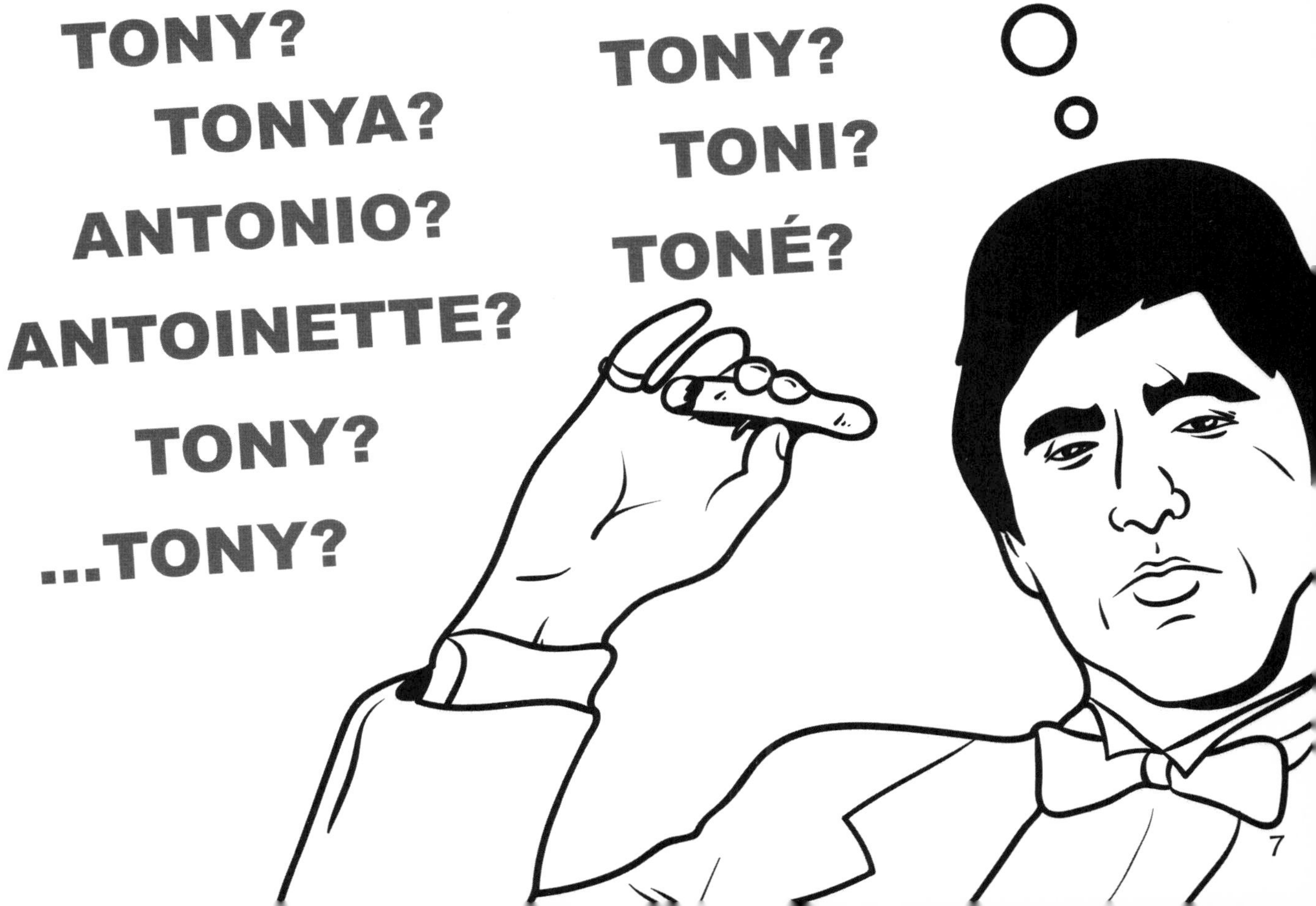
TONY?
TONYA?
ANTONIO?
ANTOINETTE?
TONY?
...TONY?
TONY?
TONI?
TONÉ?

Answers: Money, Respect, Power, Cocaine. What's that spell? Tony.

TONY PLAYS IT SAFE

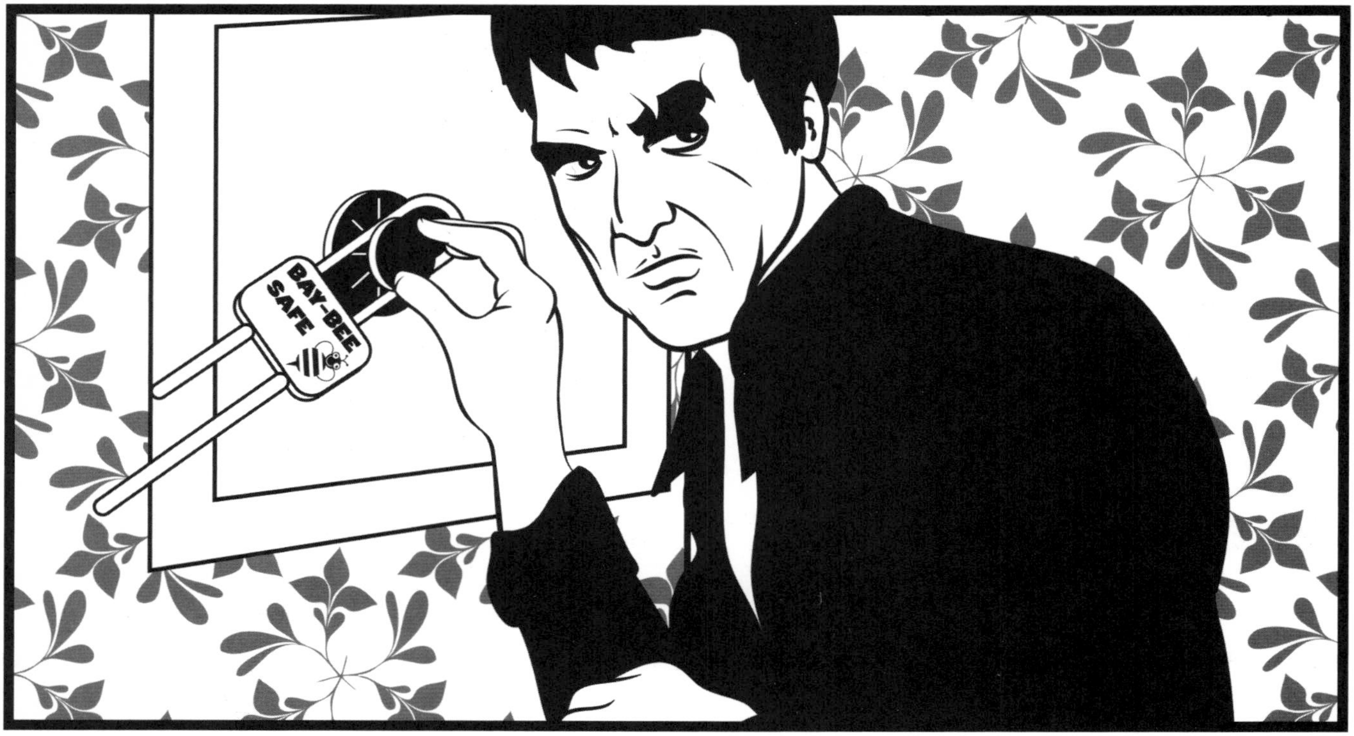
BAY-BEE SAFE

Listen. Tony Montana (oops, I mean "Joe Normalman") knows a thing or two about safety. But protecting jourself from cartel cockroaches and protecting jour baby from a boo-boo are two different things.

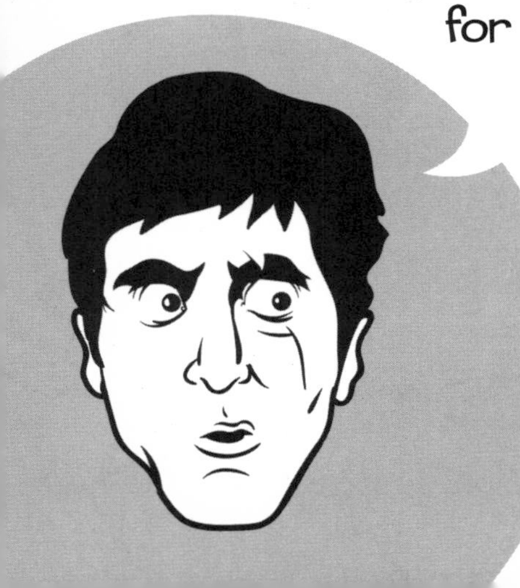

So now I gotta go out and buy all this "babyproofing" shit, mang. Locks for the toilet. Locks for the cabinet. It's like I gotta know a secret handshake just to take a shit or eat some fuckin' Crunch Berries around here. My whole house, wrapped up like a padded cell – I even put covers on the electric sockets! What kind of fucking maniac sticks his finger in a socket, mang? I don't trust this baby.

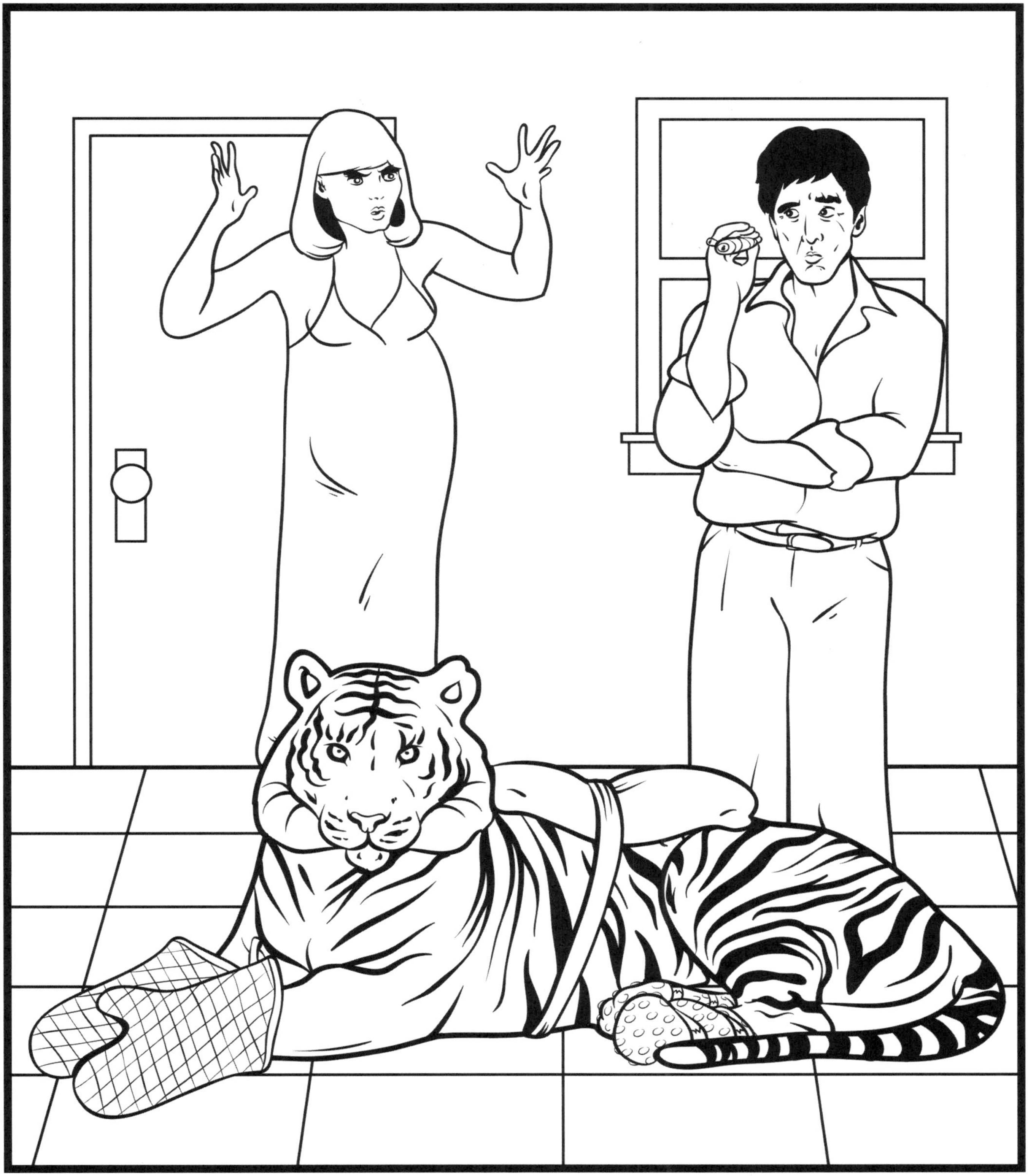

Elvira says my pet tiger is no good for the baby.
So, I babyproof it. Marriage is about compromise, mang.

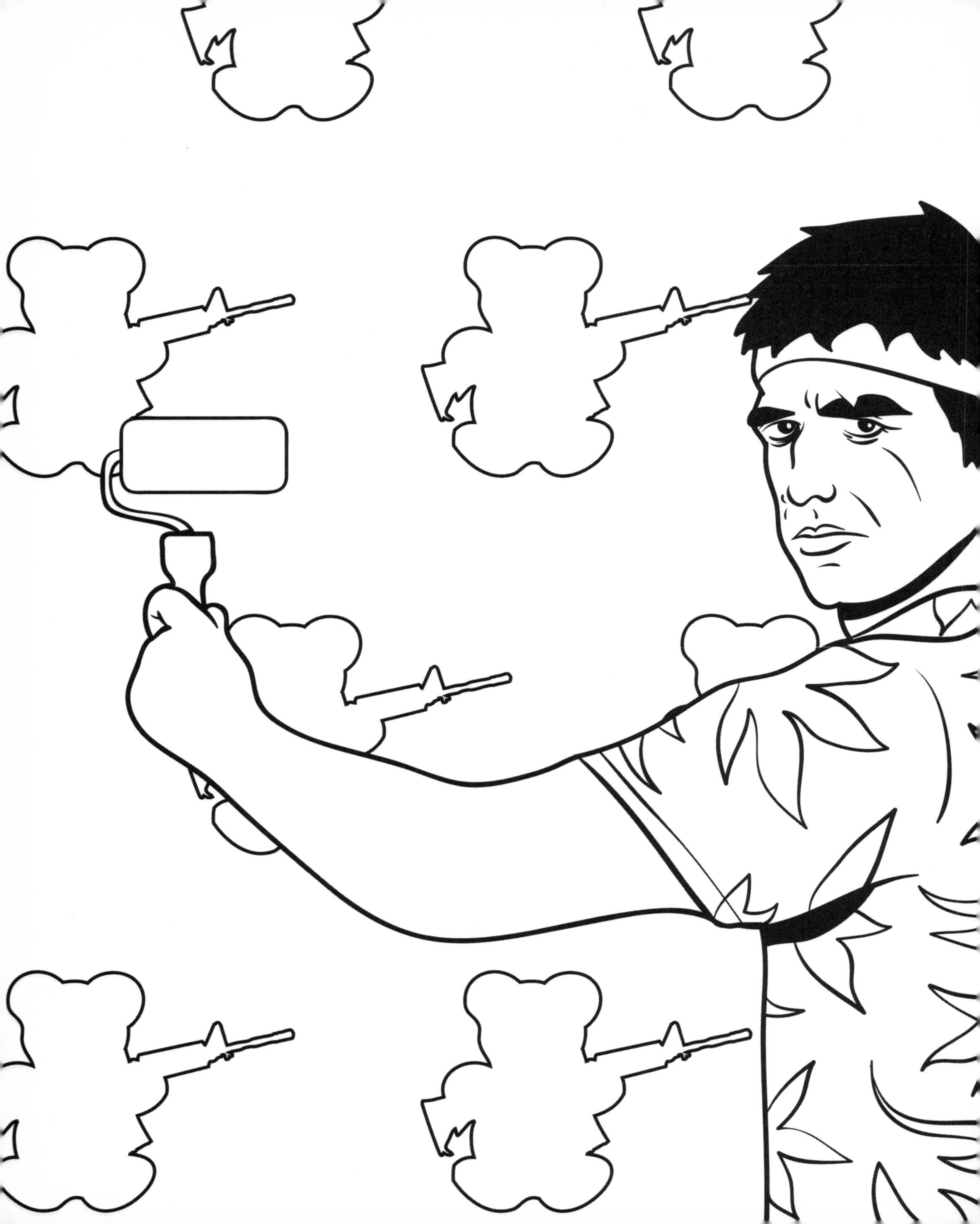

DRESS FOR SUCCESS

What do all these other dads got that I don't have? Look at the way they dress, mang. Come on. That's style. Flash, pizzazz. Socks with sandals. Cell phone belt holsters. With the right outfit, I could go straight to the top.

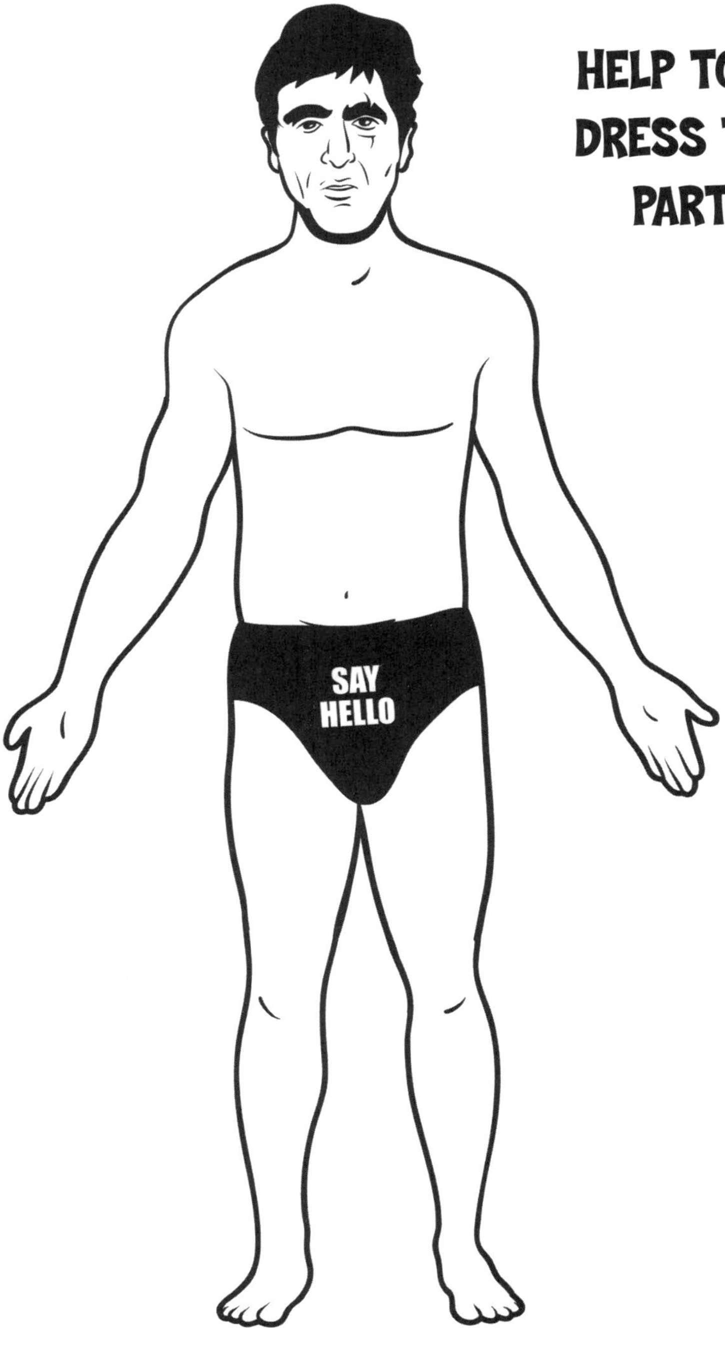
SAY
HELLO

HELP TONY DRESS THE PART!

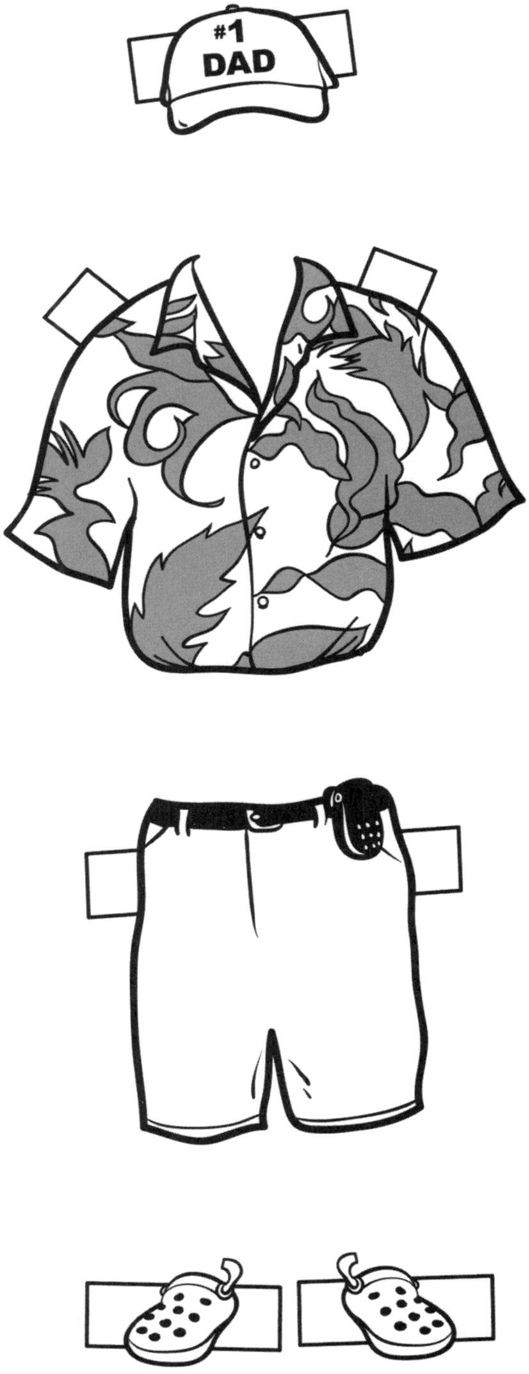
#1
DAD

PUSH IT TO THE LIMIT

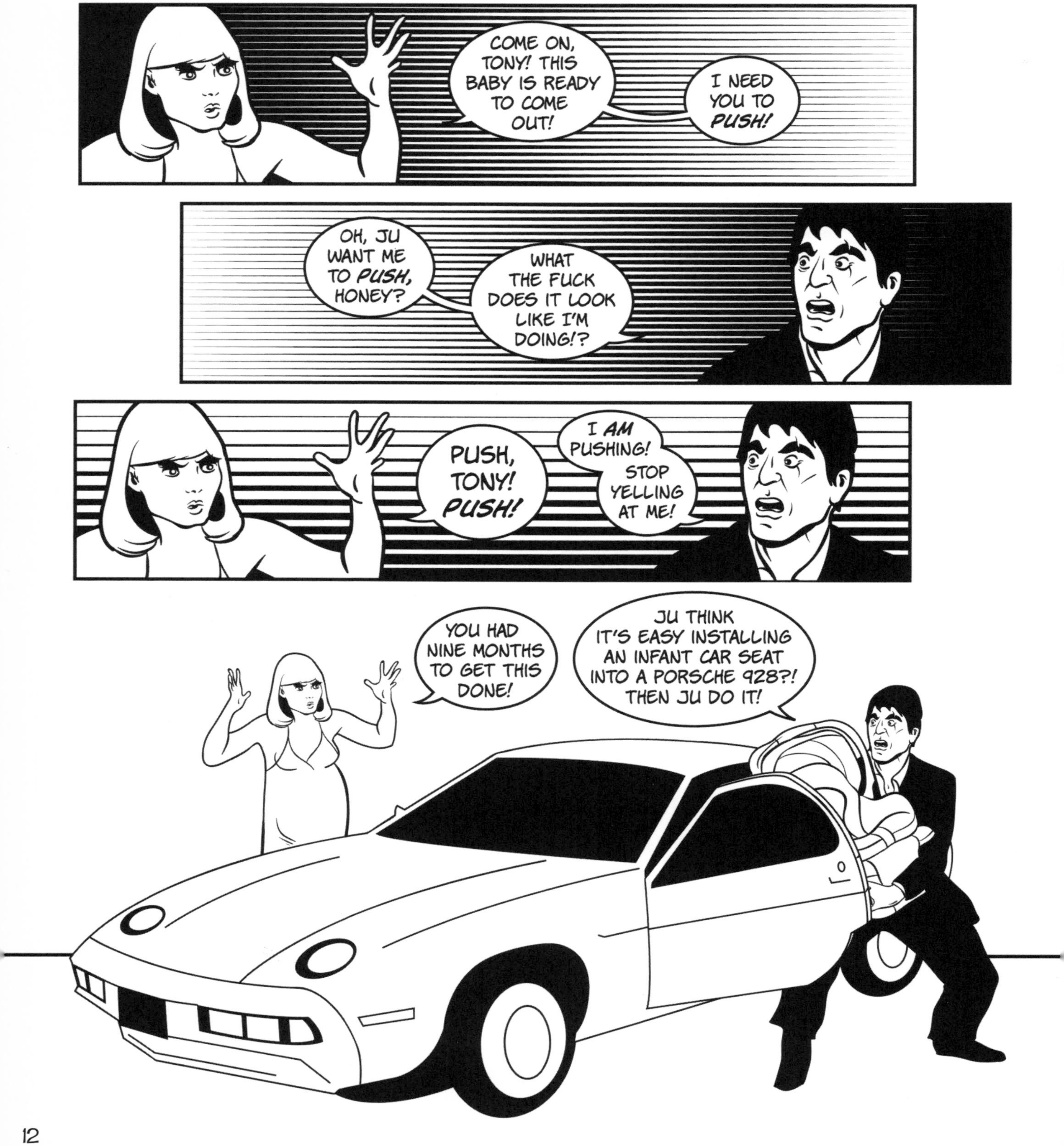
COME ON, TONY! THIS BABY IS READY TO COME OUT!
I NEED YOU TO *PUSH!*
OH, JU WANT ME TO *PUSH,* HONEY?
WHAT THE FUCK DOES IT LOOK LIKE I'M DOING!?
PUSH, TONY! *PUSH!*
I *AM* PUSHING!
STOP YELLING AT ME!
YOU HAD NINE MONTHS TO GET THIS DONE!
JU THINK IT'S EASY INSTALLING AN INFANT CAR SEAT INTO A PORSCHE 928?! THEN JU DO IT!

LET'S MAKE A DEAL

So we gotta swing by the car dealership on the way to the hospital.
But the car salesman wanna play games.
Okay, I play with *him*.

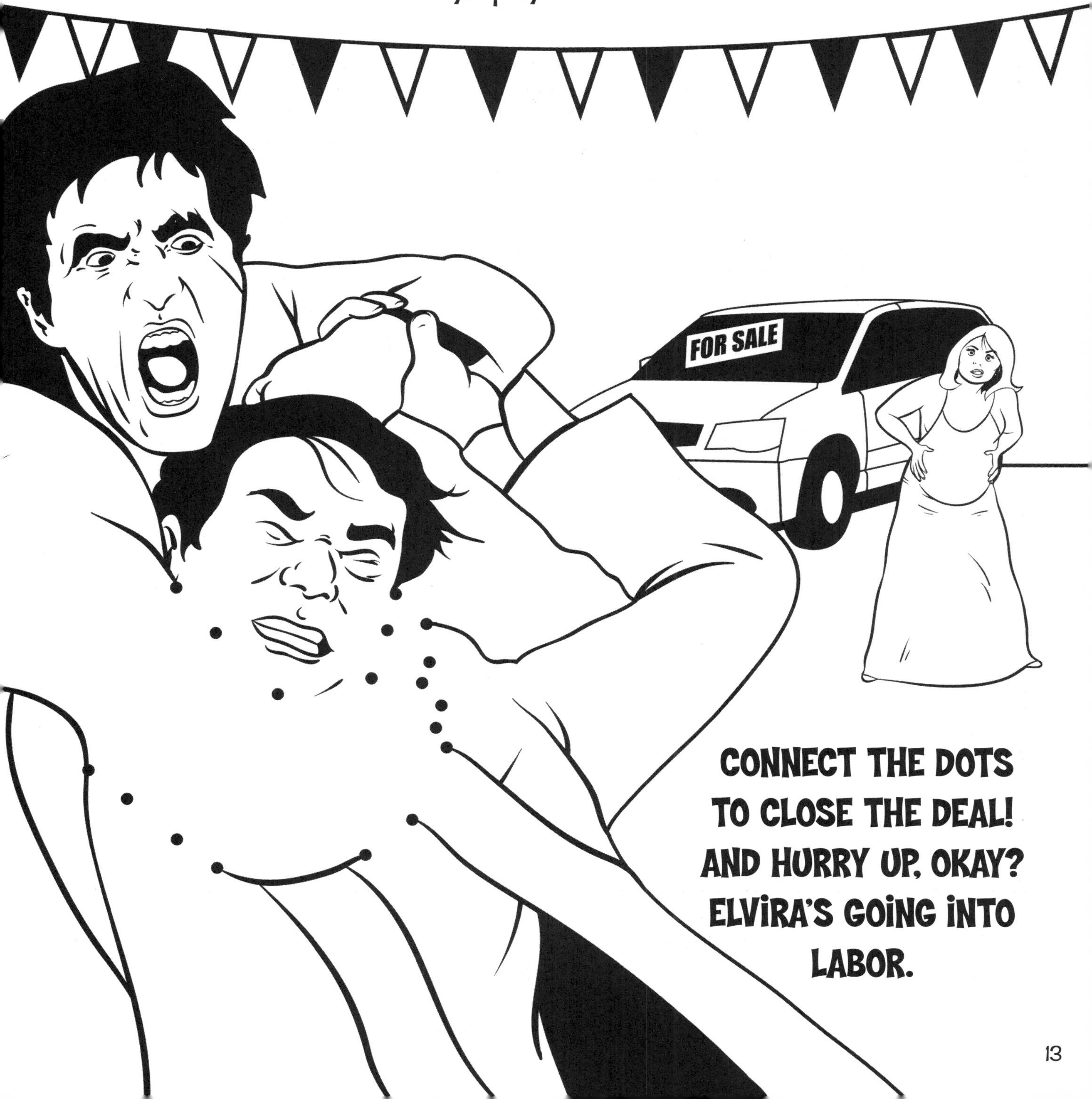
FOR SALE

CONNECT THE DOTS TO CLOSE THE DEAL! AND HURRY UP, OKAY? ELVIRA'S GOING INTO LABOR.

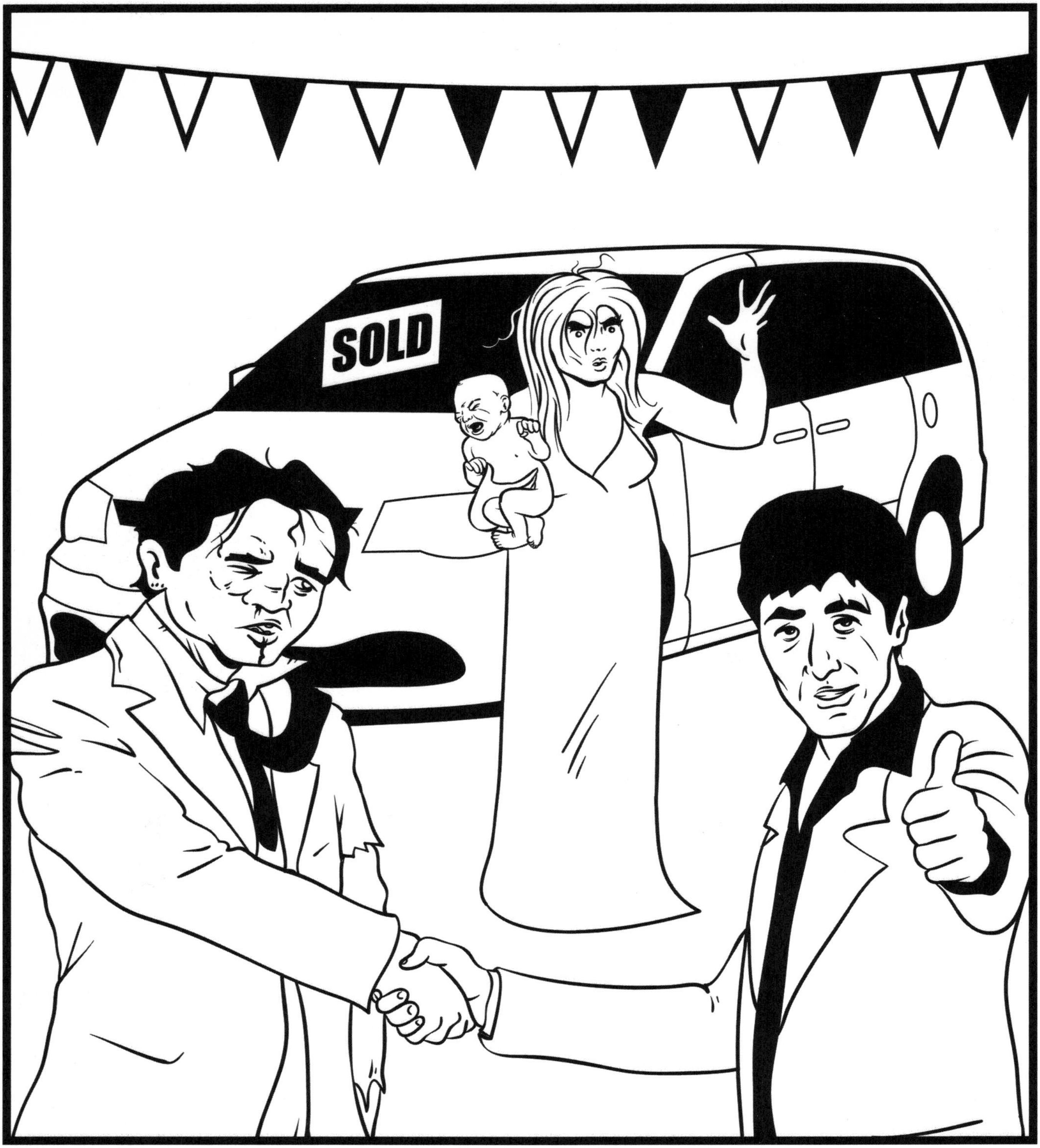
SOLD

Not only did that cockroach toss in free XM radio, but Elvira had the baby right there in the car lot, so we didn't even have to pay for a hospital. Ju fuck with Tony Montana, ju fuck with the best.

Say Hello to Our Little Friend

MR. AND MRS. JOE NORMALMAN
~PROUDLY ANNOUNCE~
THE BIRTH OF THEIR SON

Antonio Raimundo Montana, Jr.

WEIGHING 3.5 KILOS

ONE BiG HAPPY FAMiLY

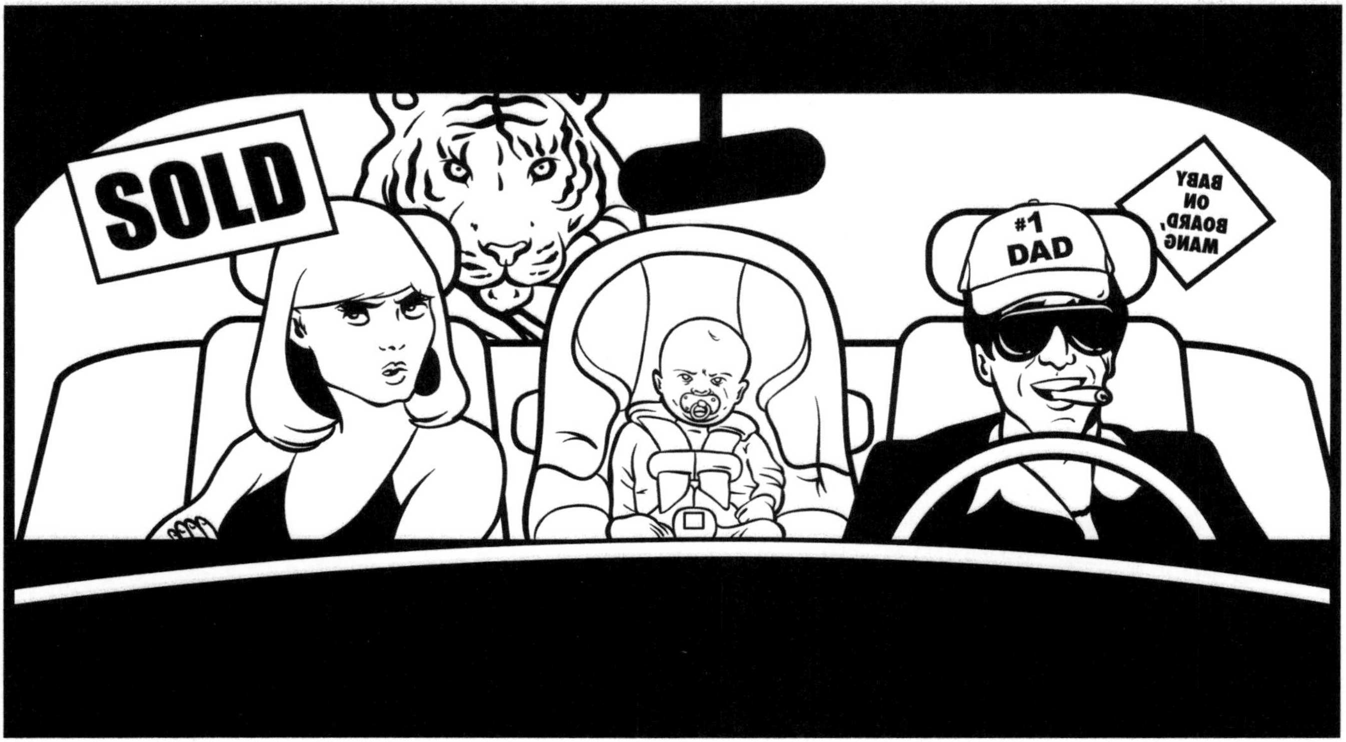
SOLD
#1 DAD
BABY ON BOARD, MANG

Ju know, becoming a father really changes everything. Before Little Antonio came along, my priorities were all fucked up, mang. But now I'm just focusing on being a dad... and being a new minivan owner! This thing came with GPS, a DVD player, and cup holders like a motherfucker. Seriously, mang. Who even owns this many cups. It's ridiculous.

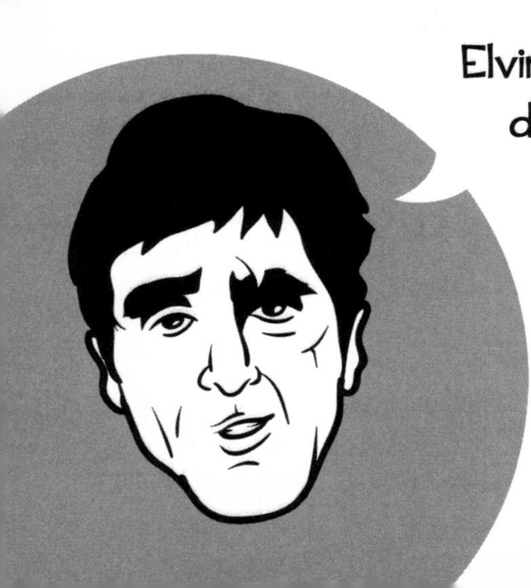

Elvira got a job at a law firm (all this time she had a doctorate in juridicial science, who knew?) so that means I'm gonna have to take care of the little guy all by myself. That's right, Tony Montana just became a stay at home dad.

And I'm gonna be the best fucking stay at home dad ever.

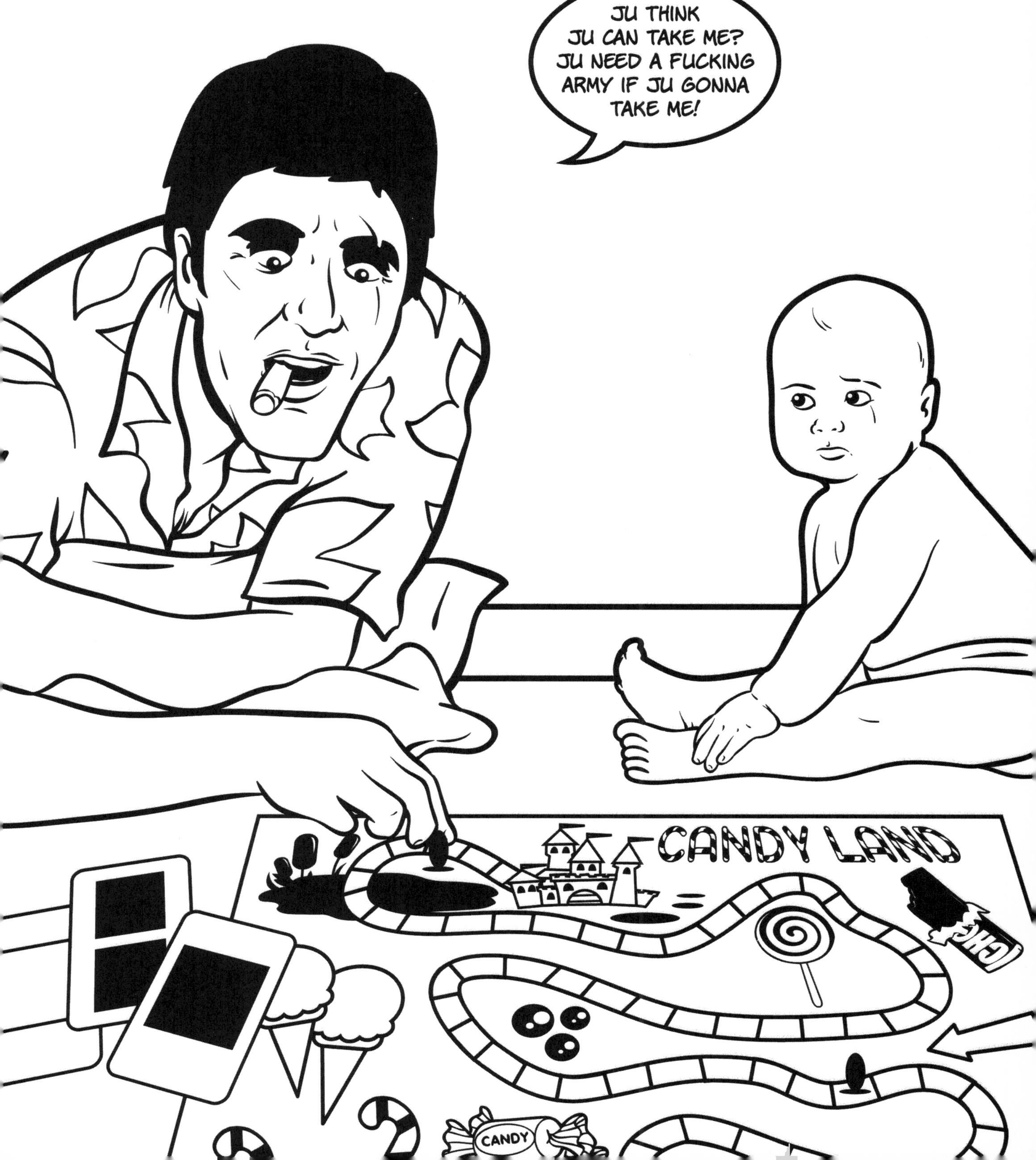
JU THINK JU CAN TAKE ME? JU NEED A FUCKING ARMY IF JU GONNA TAKE ME!
CANDY LAND
CANDY

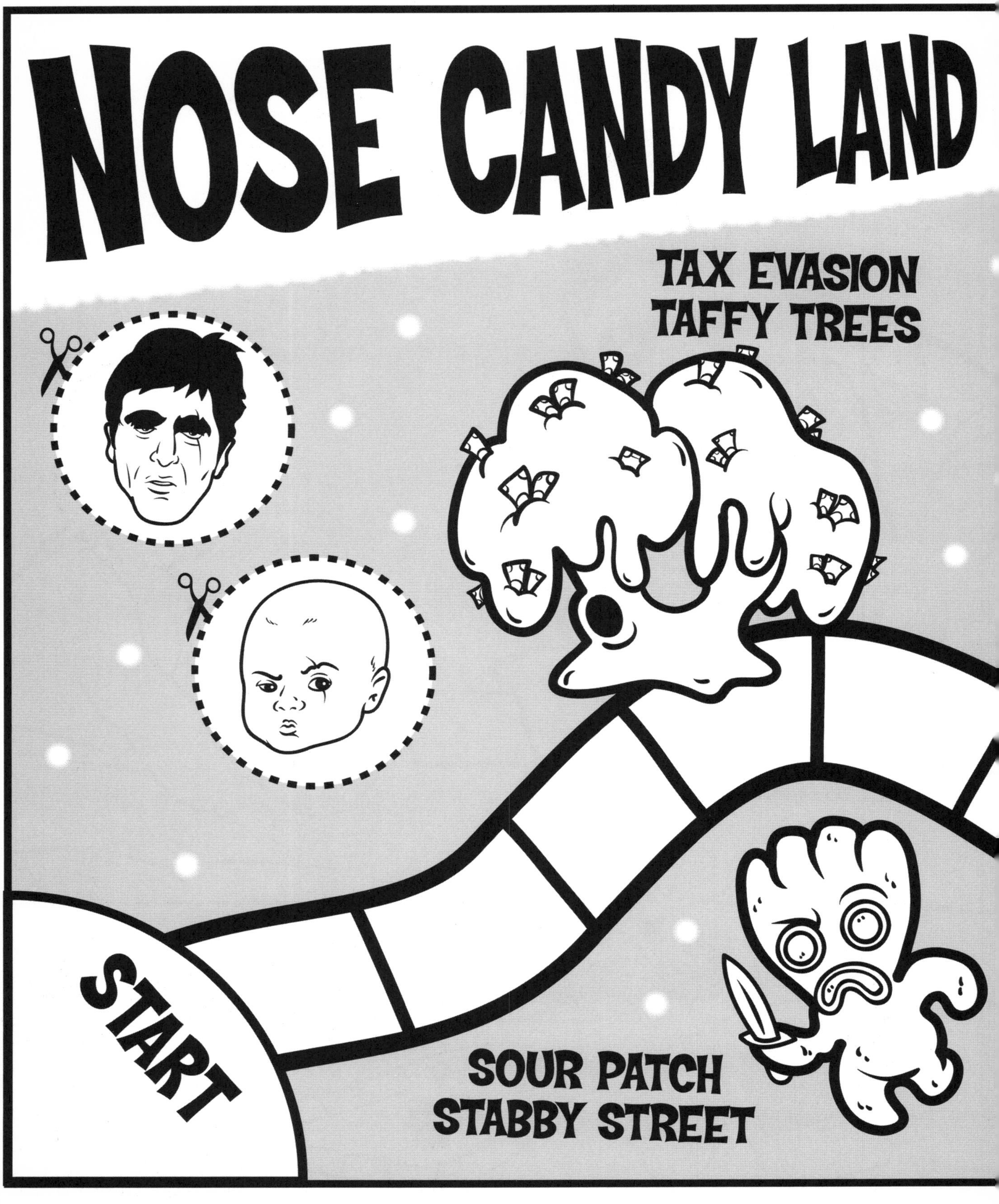
NOSE CANDY LAND
TAX EVASION
TAFFY TREES
START
SOUR PATCH
STABBY STREET

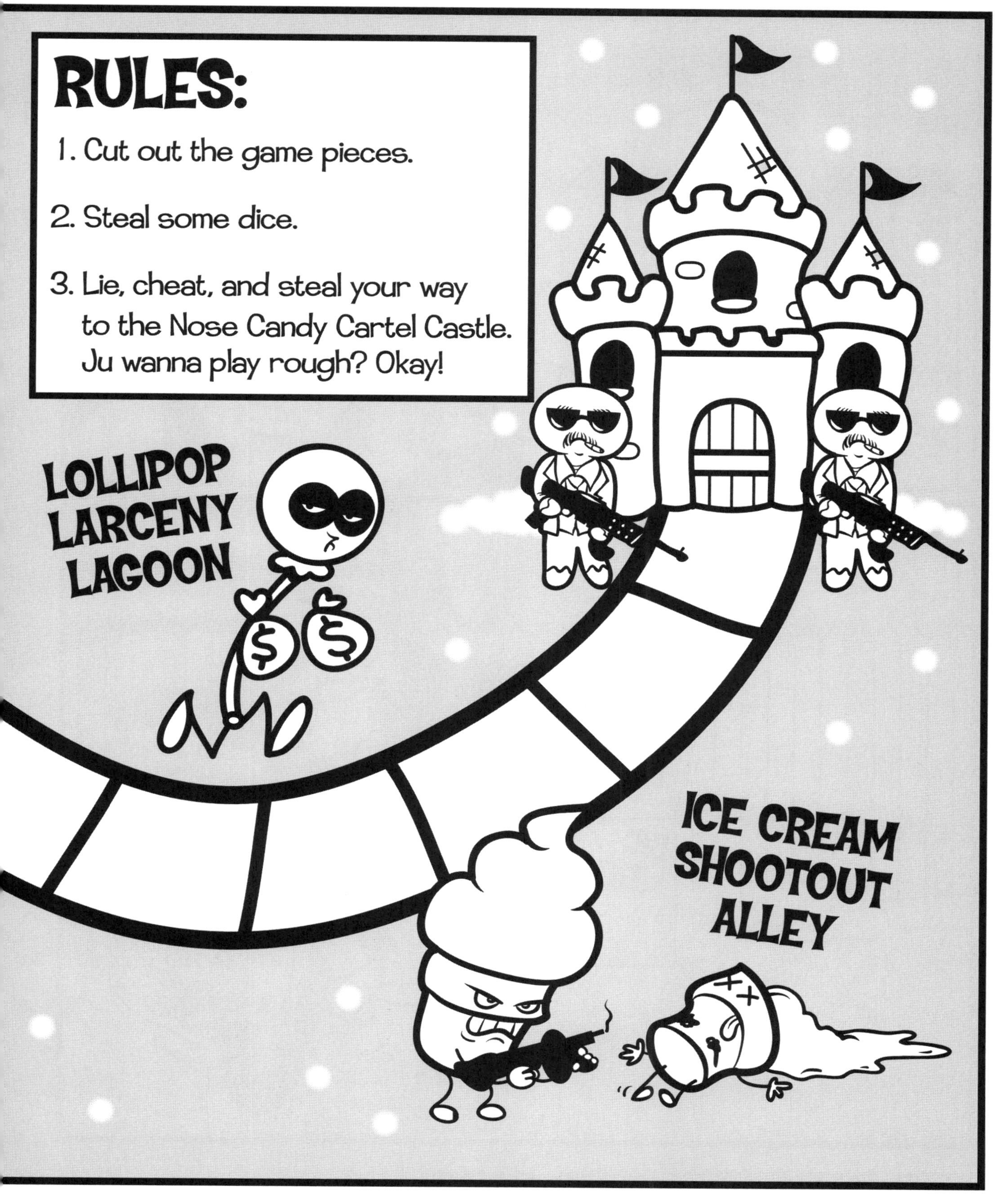
RULES:
1. Cut out the game pieces.
2. Steal some dice.
3. Lie, cheat, and steal your way to the Nose Candy Cartel Castle. Ju wanna play rough? Okay!
LOLLIPOP LARCENY LAGOON
ICE CREAM SHOOTOUT ALLEY

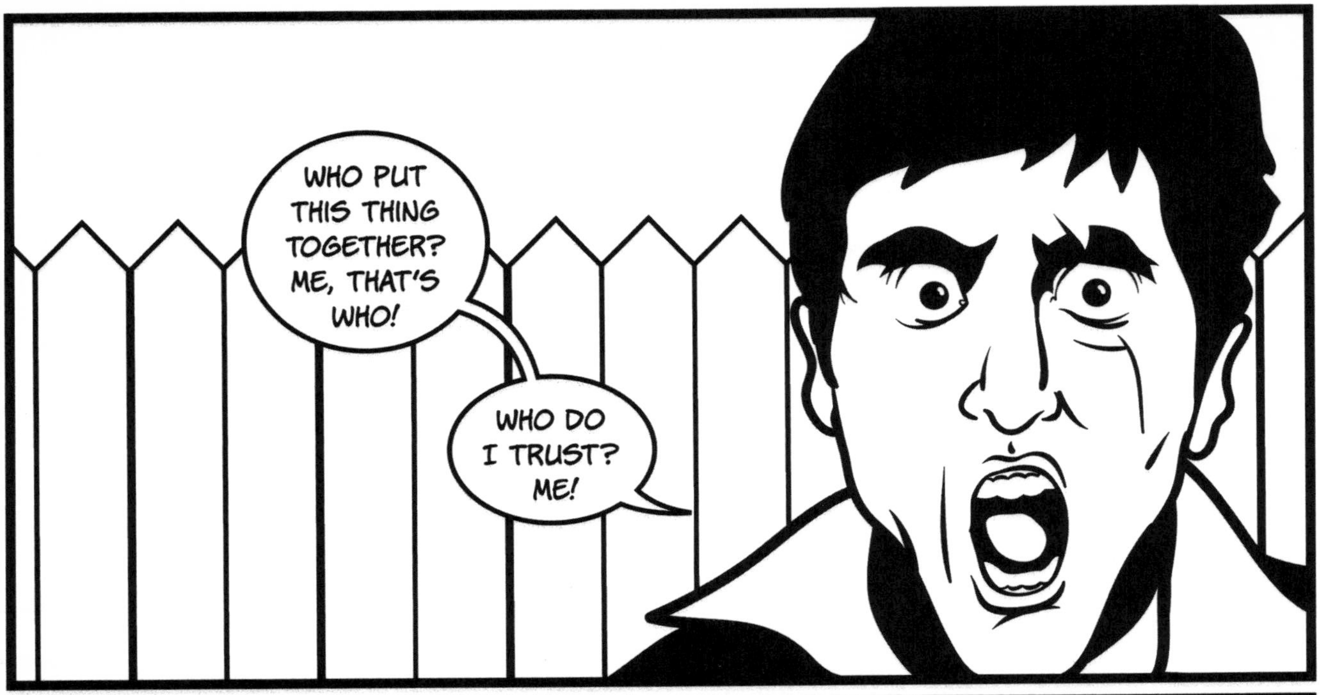
WHO PUT THIS THING TOGETHER? ME, THAT'S WHO!
WHO DO I TRUST? ME!

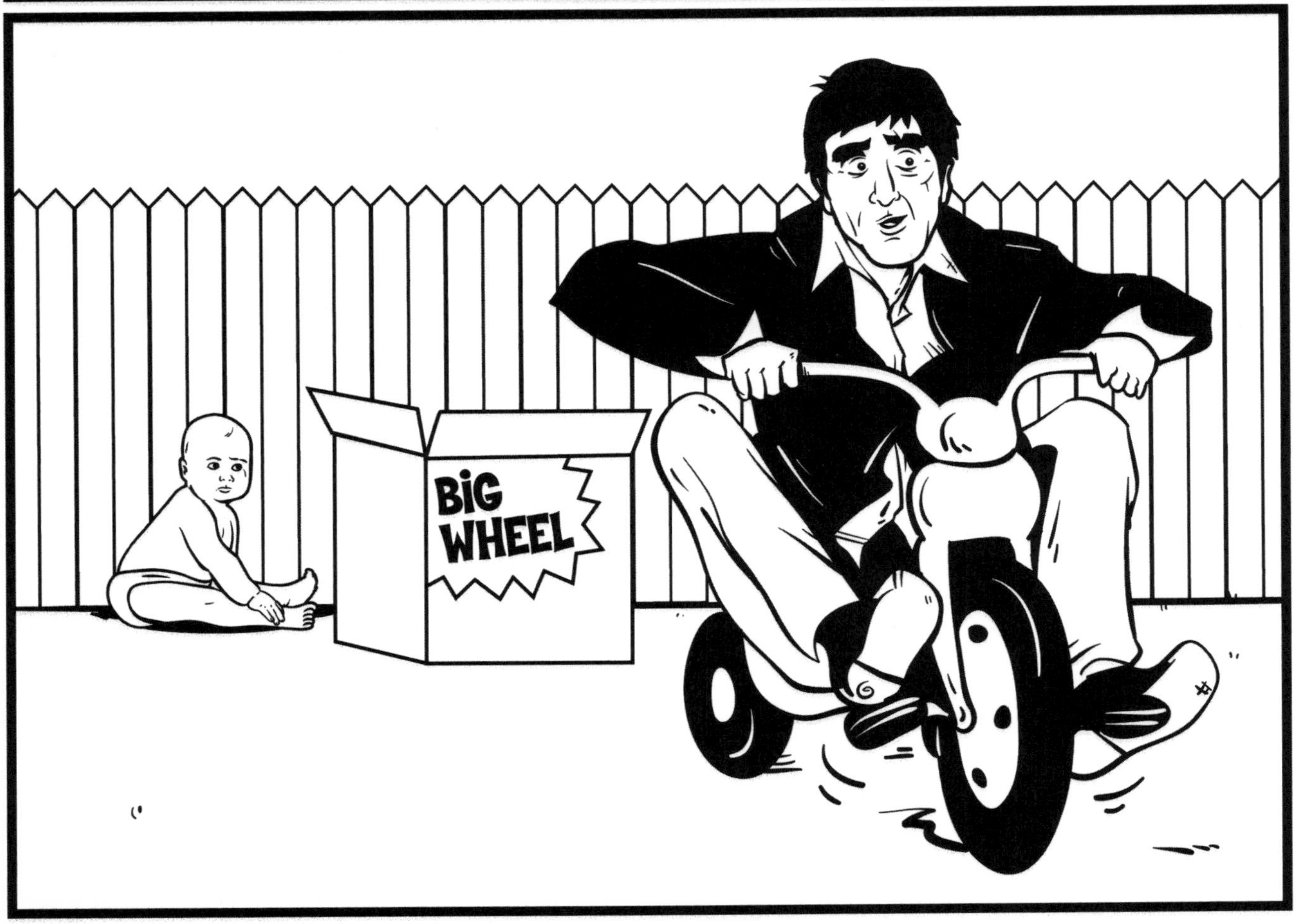
BIG WHEEL

I buy him toys.

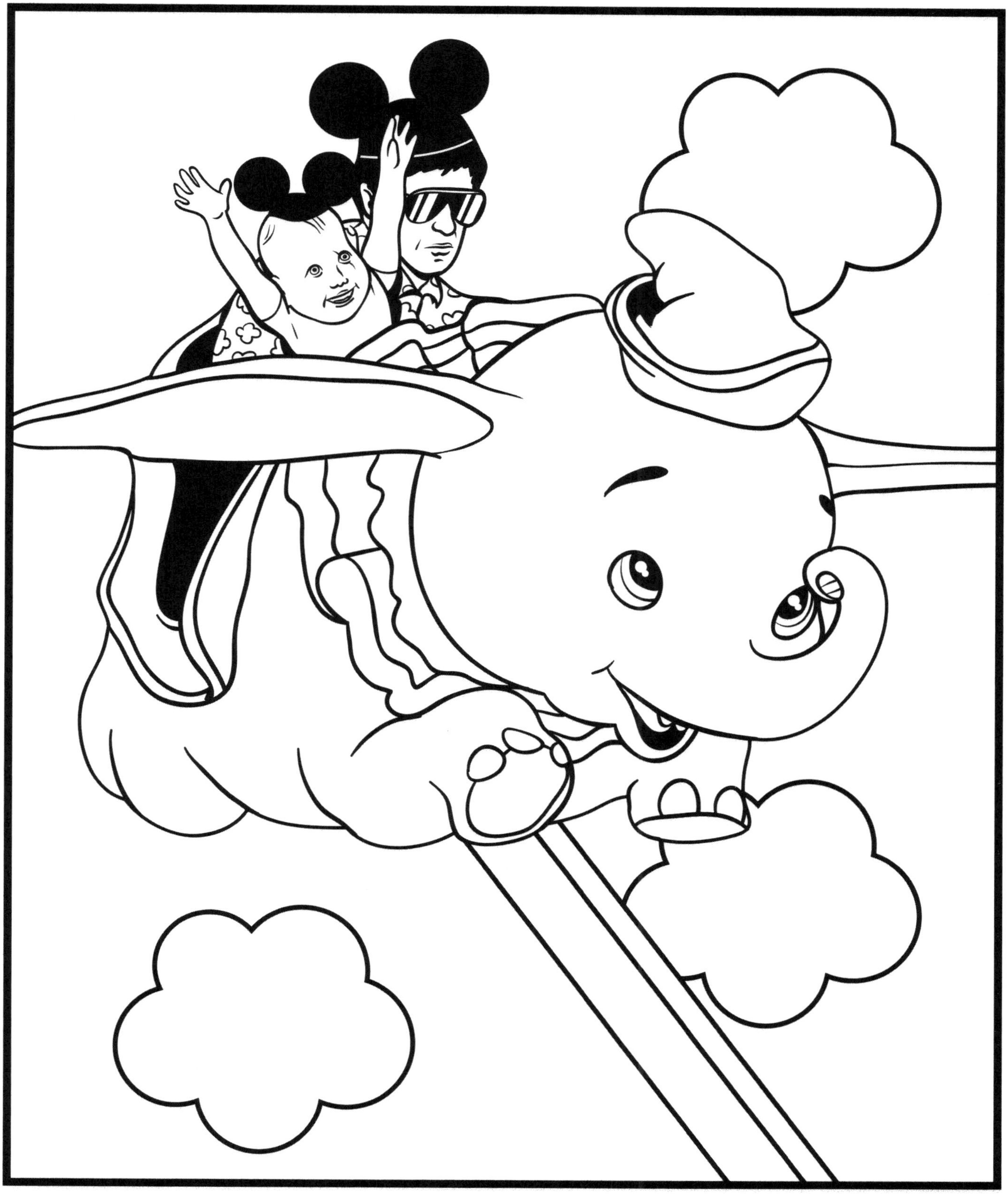

I even take him to Dummyland.

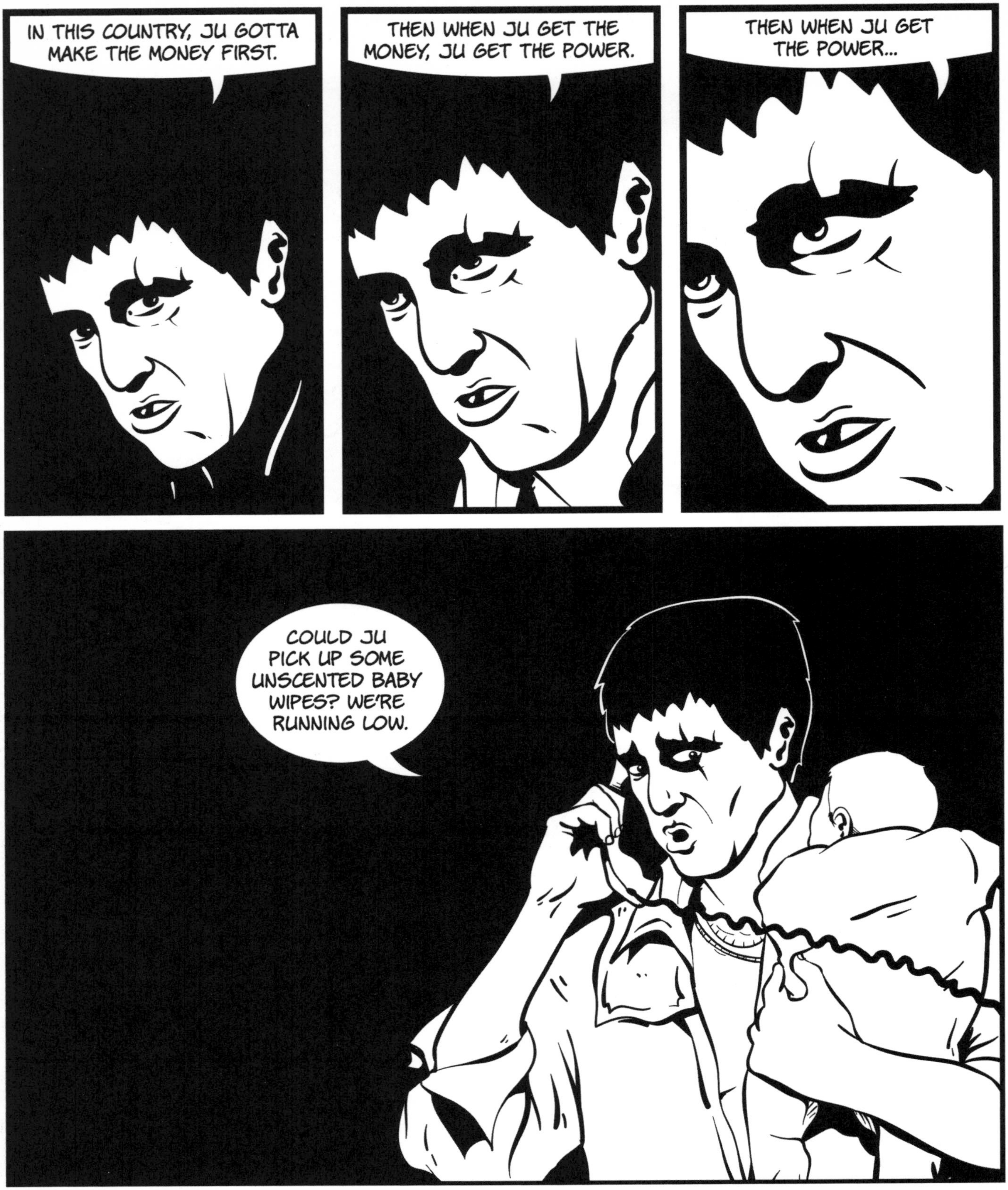
IN THIS COUNTRY, JU GOTTA MAKE THE MONEY FIRST.
THEN WHEN JU GET THE MONEY, JU GET THE POWER.
THEN WHEN JU GET THE POWER...
COULD JU PICK UP SOME UNSCENTED BABY WIPES? WE'RE RUNNING LOW.

It gets expensive, mang. I'm spending more on baby supplies than I ever did on cocaine.

TONY GOES SHOPPING

"Super center," my ass. I been in refugee camps
that were more organized than this dump!

```
F  U  C  K  S  H  I  T  B  I  B  S  D  I  E
O  K  I  L  L  M  U  R  D  E  R  F  U  C  K
R  B  L  A  N  K  E  T  D  I  E  S  H  I  T
M  U  R  D  E  R  S  O  C  K  S  D  I  E  B
U  D  I  A  P  E  R  S  D  I  E  D  I  E  O
L  D  I  E  F  U  C  K  D  I  E  S  H  I  T
A  S  H  I  T  R  A  T  T  L  E  S  H  I  T
P  A  C  I  F  I  E  R  D  I  E  K  I  L  L
S  H  I  T  F  U  C  K  K  I  L  L  D  I  E
```

HELP TONY FIND WHAT HE NEEDS SO HE CAN GET THE HELL OUT OF HERE!

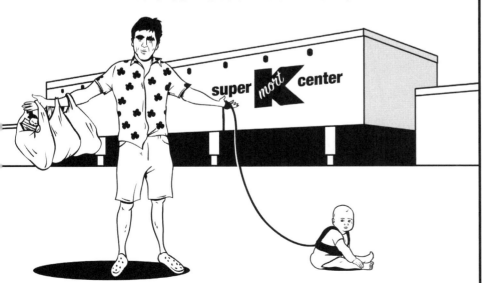

super K mort center

WORD LIST

BIBS

SOCKS

FORMULA

PACIFIER

BLANKET

BOTTLE

DIAPERS

RATTLE

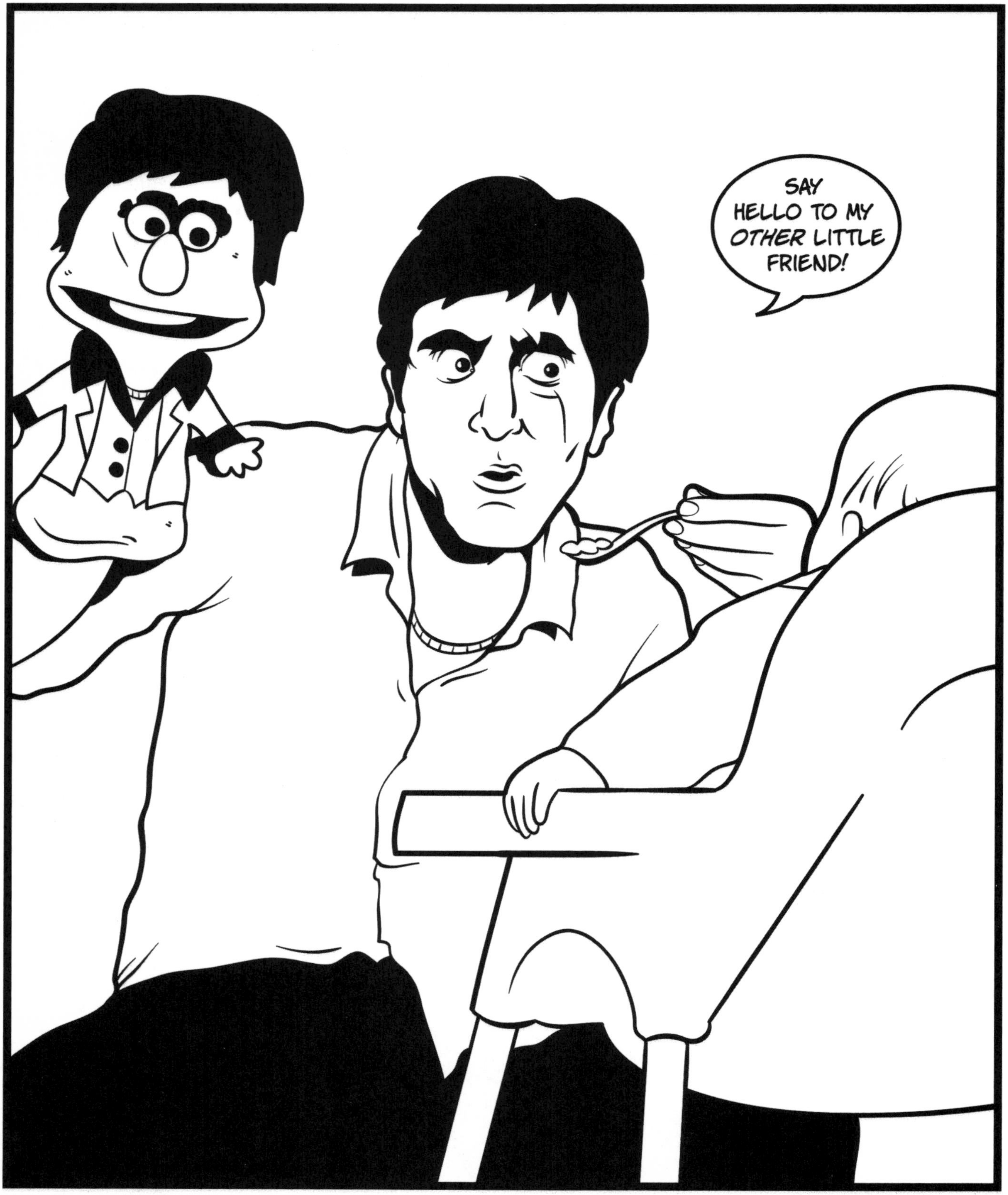
SAY HELLO TO MY *OTHER* LITTLE FRIEND!

It ain't all fun and games. Feeding him is a pain in the ass.

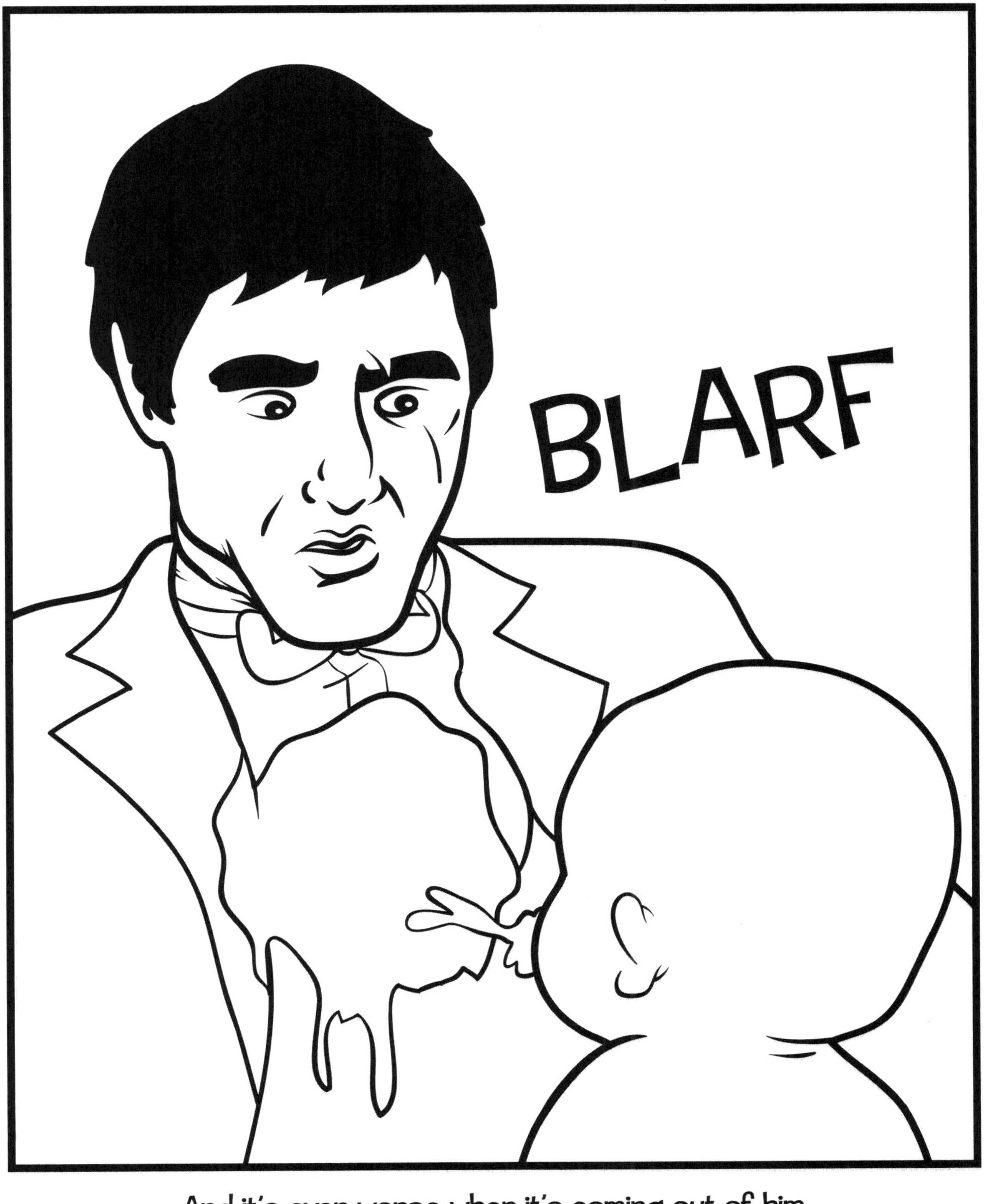
BLARF

And it's even worse when it's coming out of him.

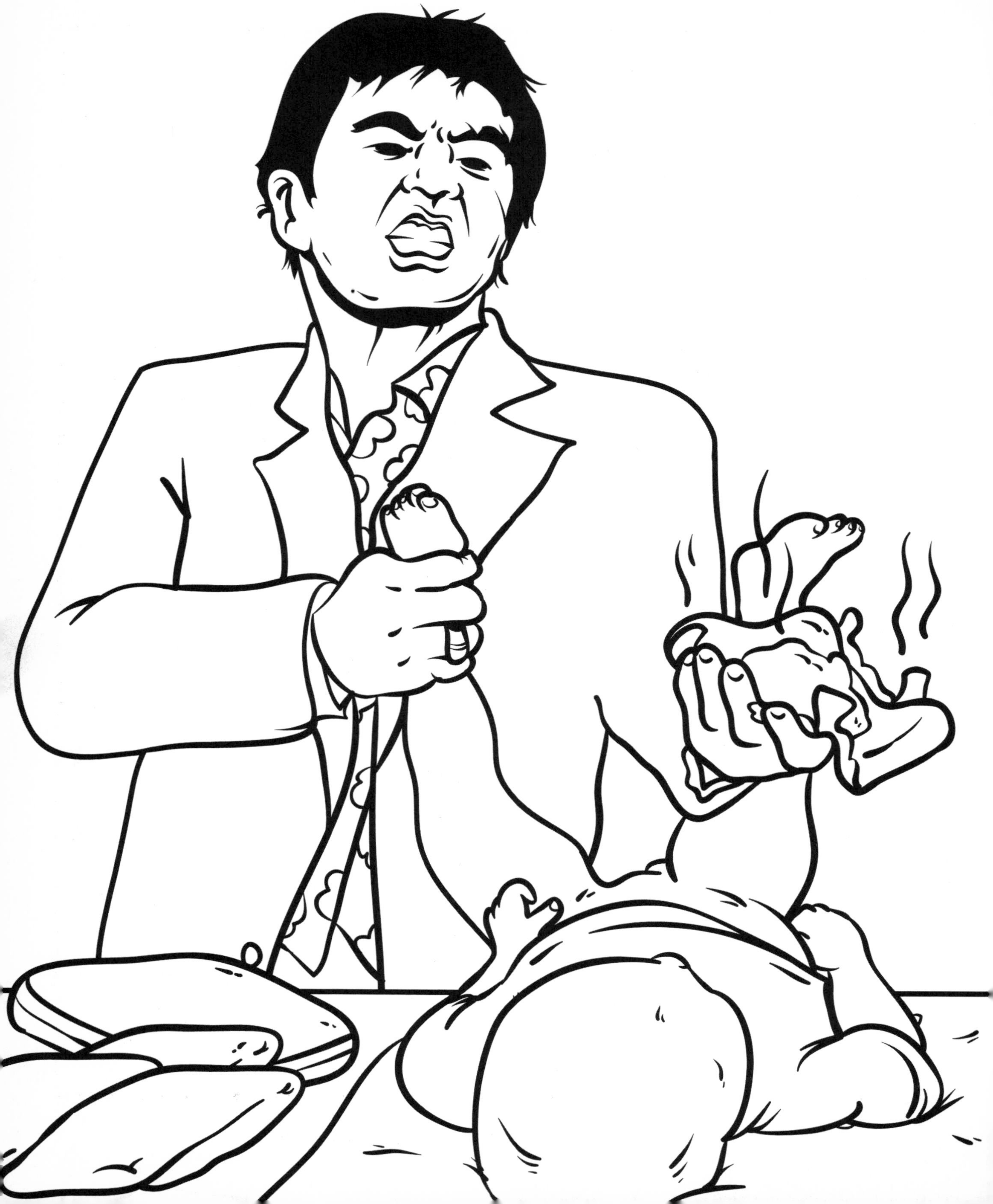

DON'T PUSH ME, BABY

The truth is, sometimes this baby can be kind of an asshole.
Always screaming his baby gibberish at me. Speak English, baby!
What do ju want?!

X OUT THE ITEMS TONY SHOULD DEFINITELY NOT GIVE TO A BABY

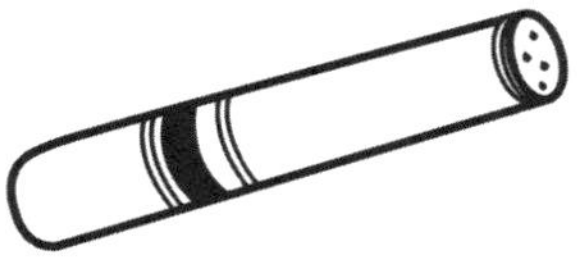

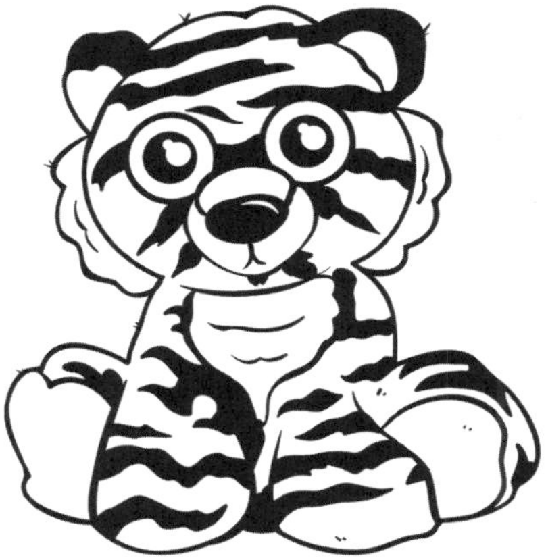

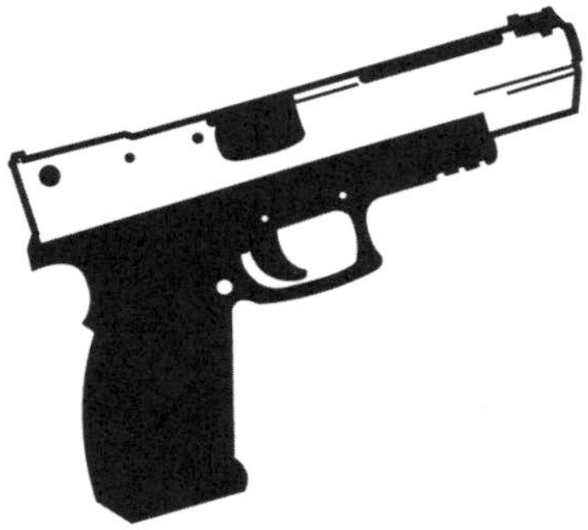

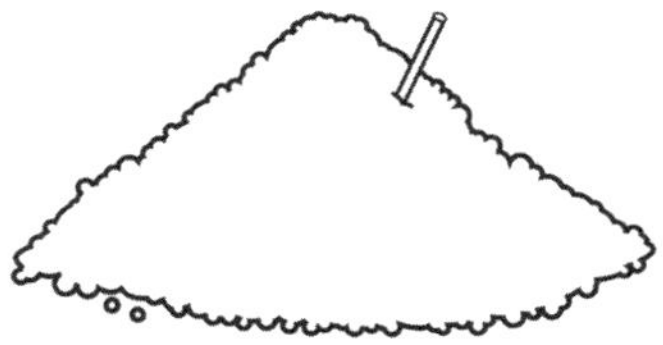

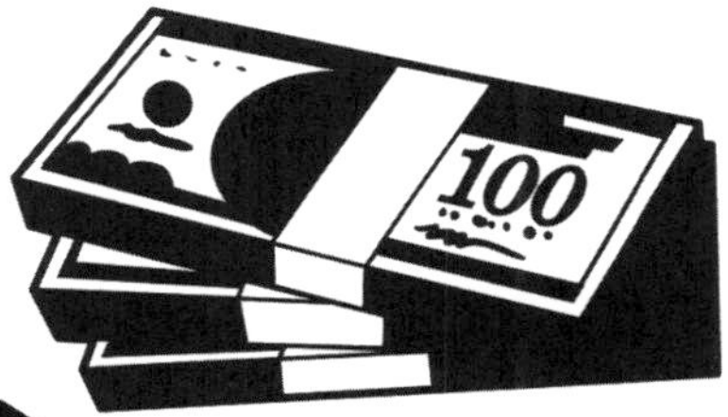
100

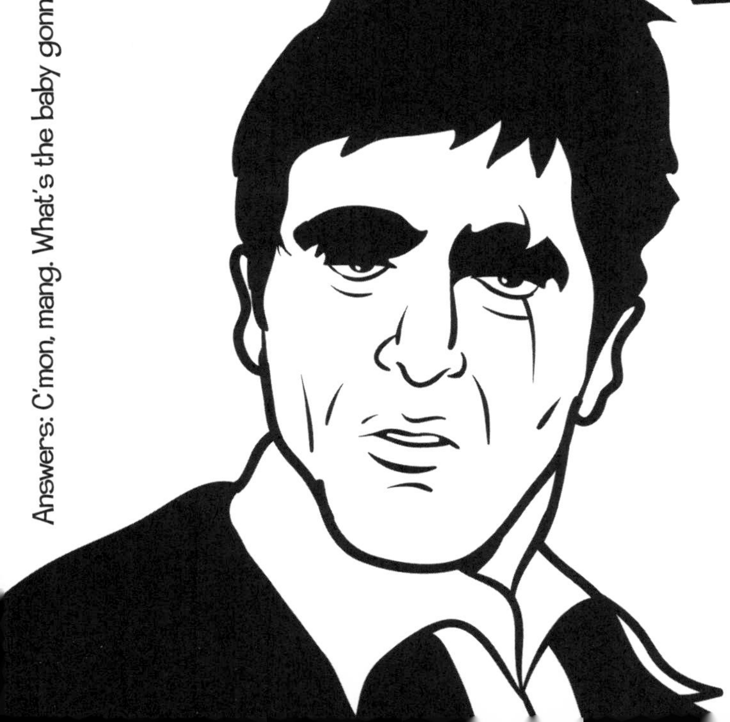

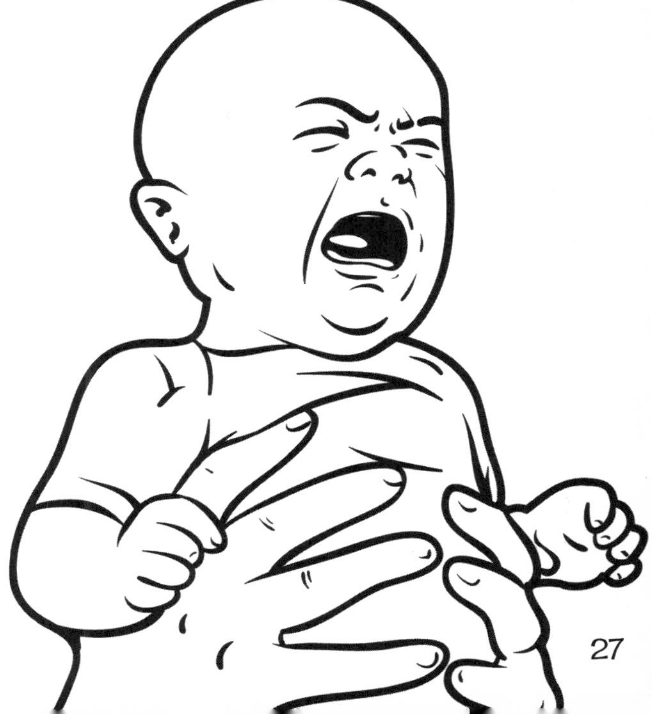

Answers: C'mon, mang. What's the baby gonna do with a pile of cash?

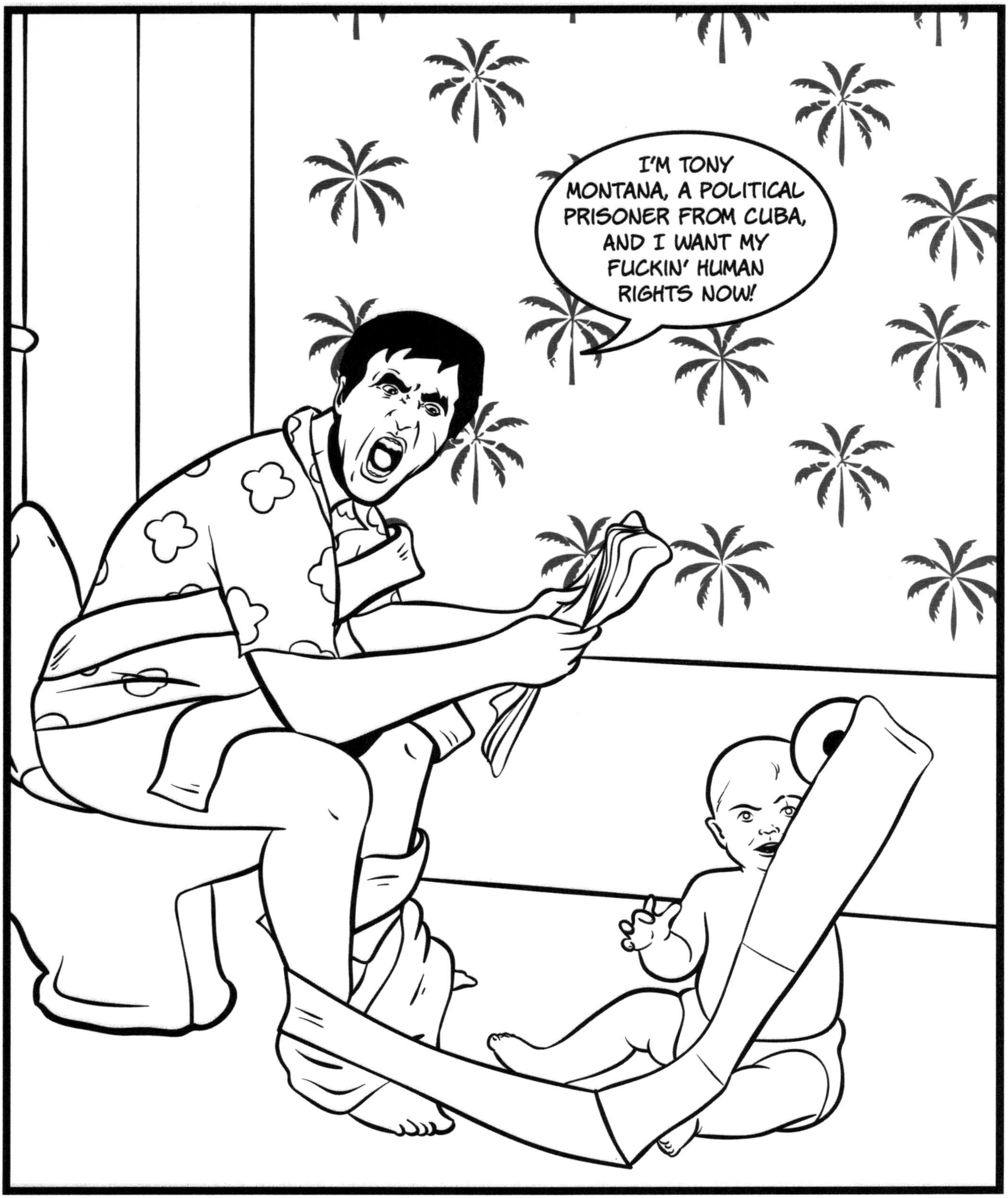
I'M TONY MONTANA, A POLITICAL PRISONER FROM CUBA, AND I WANT MY FUCKIN' HUMAN RIGHTS NOW!

I spend every fuckin' minute of my day with this kid, mang.

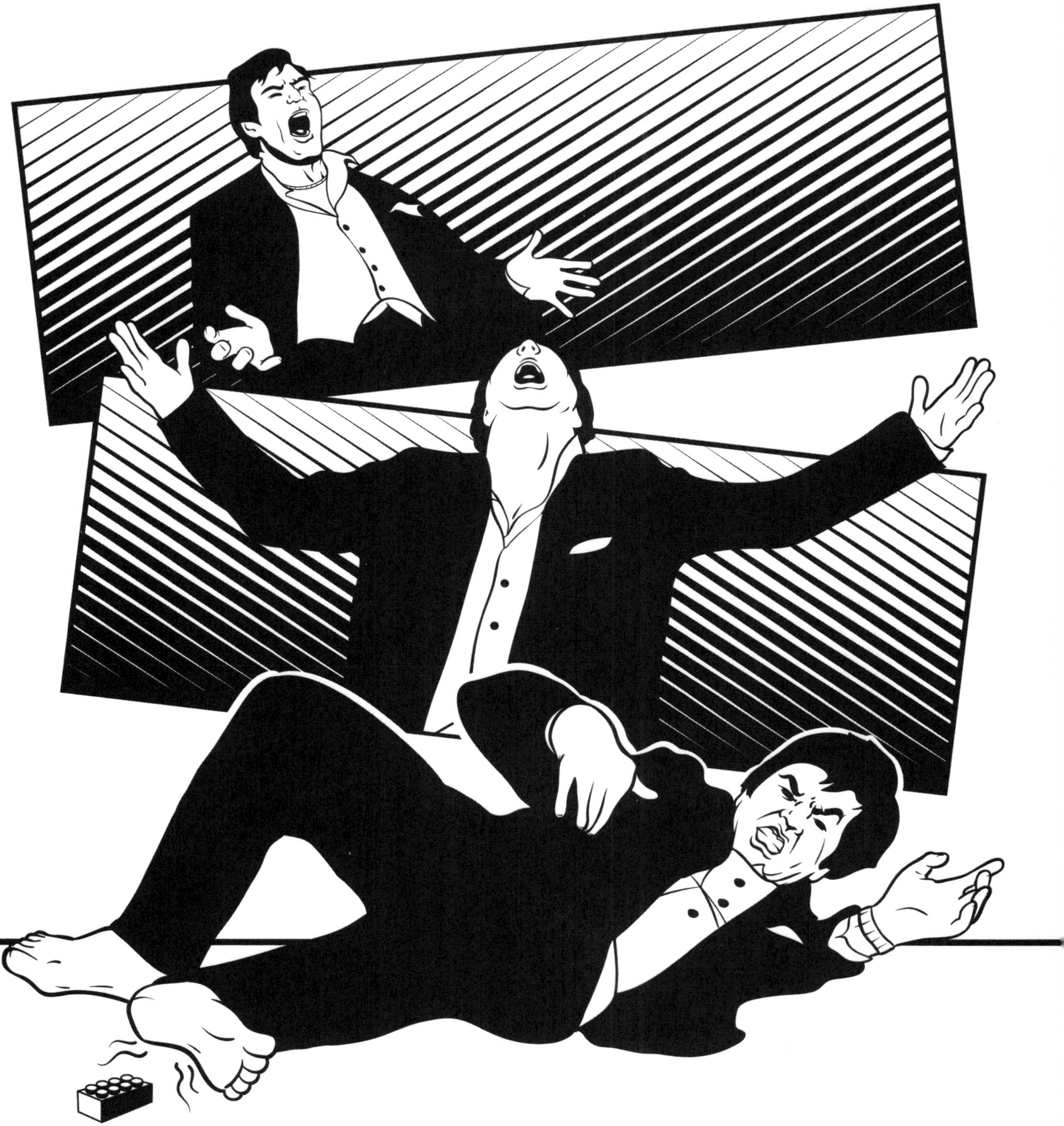

I been strangled, shot and stabbed – sometimes all at once.
Pero coño, I never knew what real pain felt like until
I stepped on a Lego barefoot!

TONY NEEDS HELP

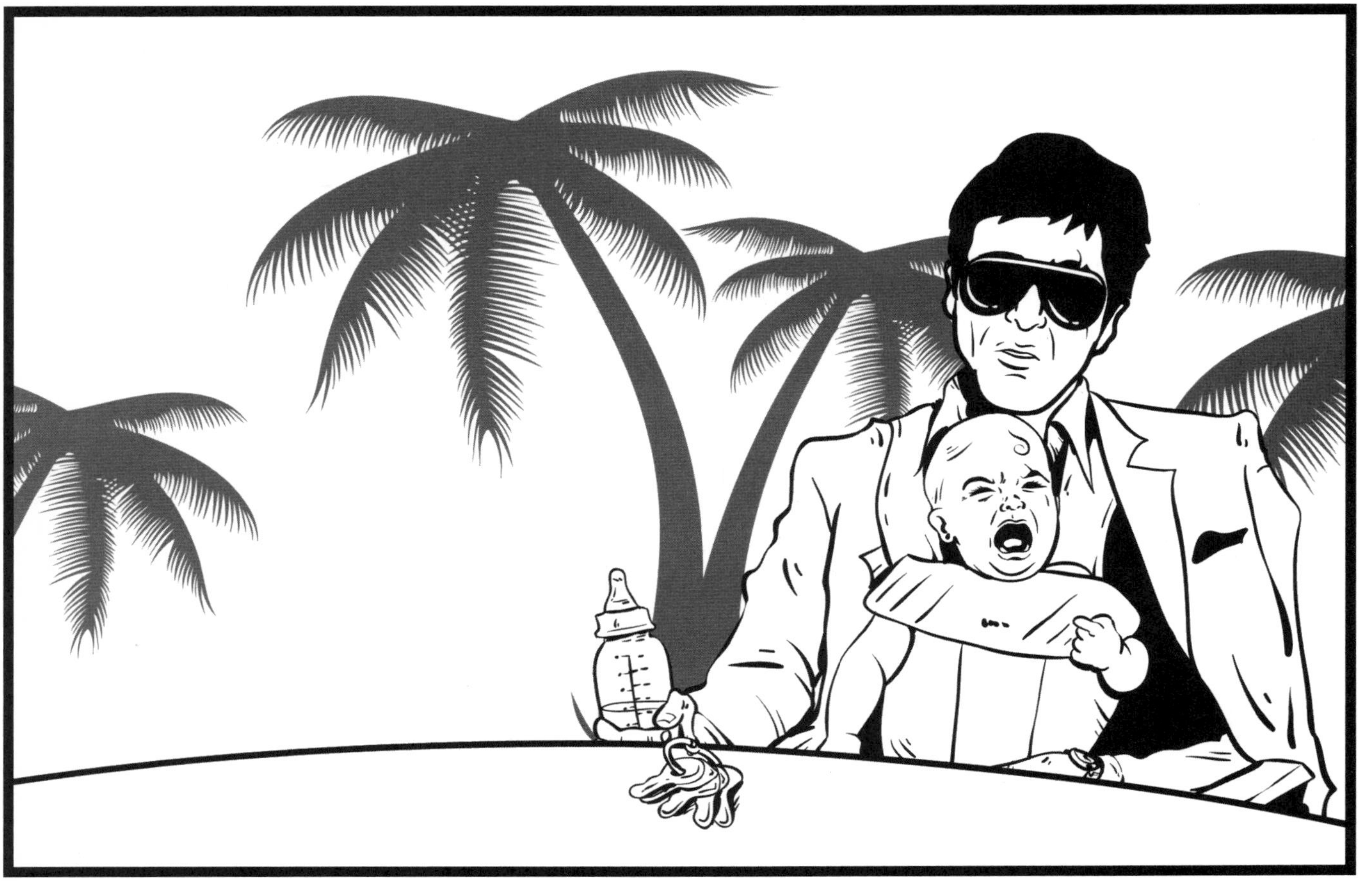

Parenting ain't no duckwalk, let me tell ju.

My back hurts. I haven't slept in months. Sometimes I'll leave the house with a dirty burp cloth on my shoulder and I won't even realize it. The other day I accidentally baby-talked a bank teller. Called him "my little tinker-doodle."

My whole fucking life is falling apart, mang.

I gotta make a move and I gotta make one quick. I gotta put this baby in daycare.

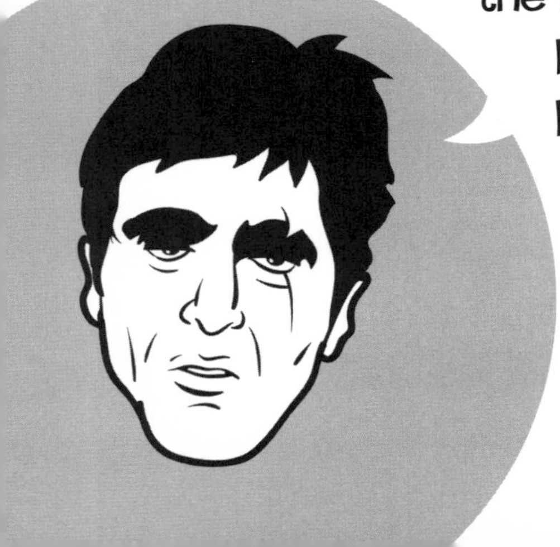

DAYCARE DiSARRAY

Just one problem: All these daycares got waiting lists a mile long, mang.
Since when ju gotta be on a list to get into a fucking daycare?
What is this, the Babylon Club?!

HELP ELViRA AND TONY FiND A DAYCARE THAT WiLL TAKE THEM!

LiTERALLY ANYTHiNG WiLL DO AT THiS POiNT!

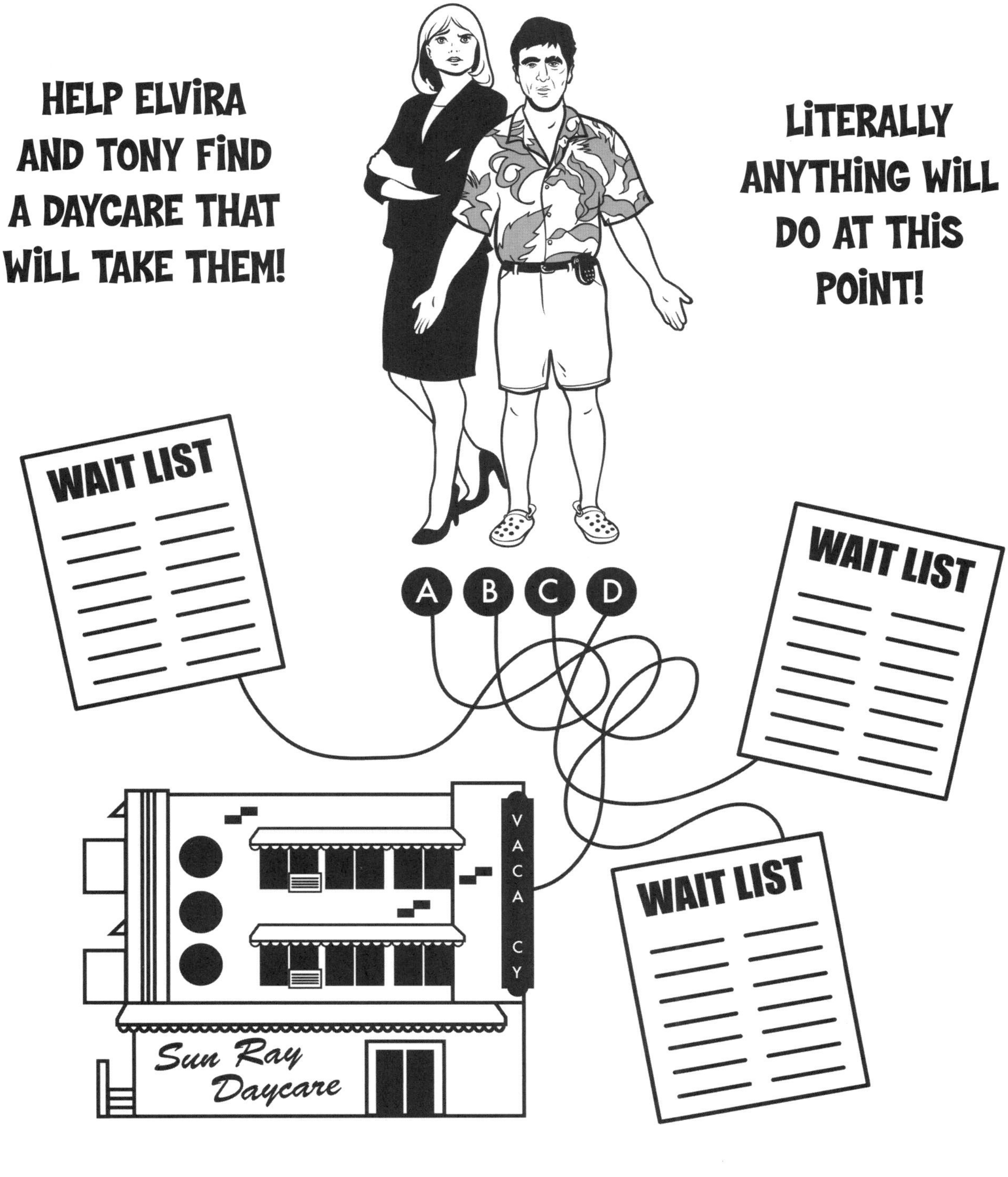
WAIT LIST
A
B
C
D
WAIT LIST
VACANCY
WAIT LIST
Sun Ray Daycare

Answer: B. No wait. I mean D. Shit, that's not it either... C? Just choose C! Hurry up, mang!

WHAT THE FUCK'S WRONG WITH THIS PICTURE

I don't know about this daycare, mang. It seems... fishy.

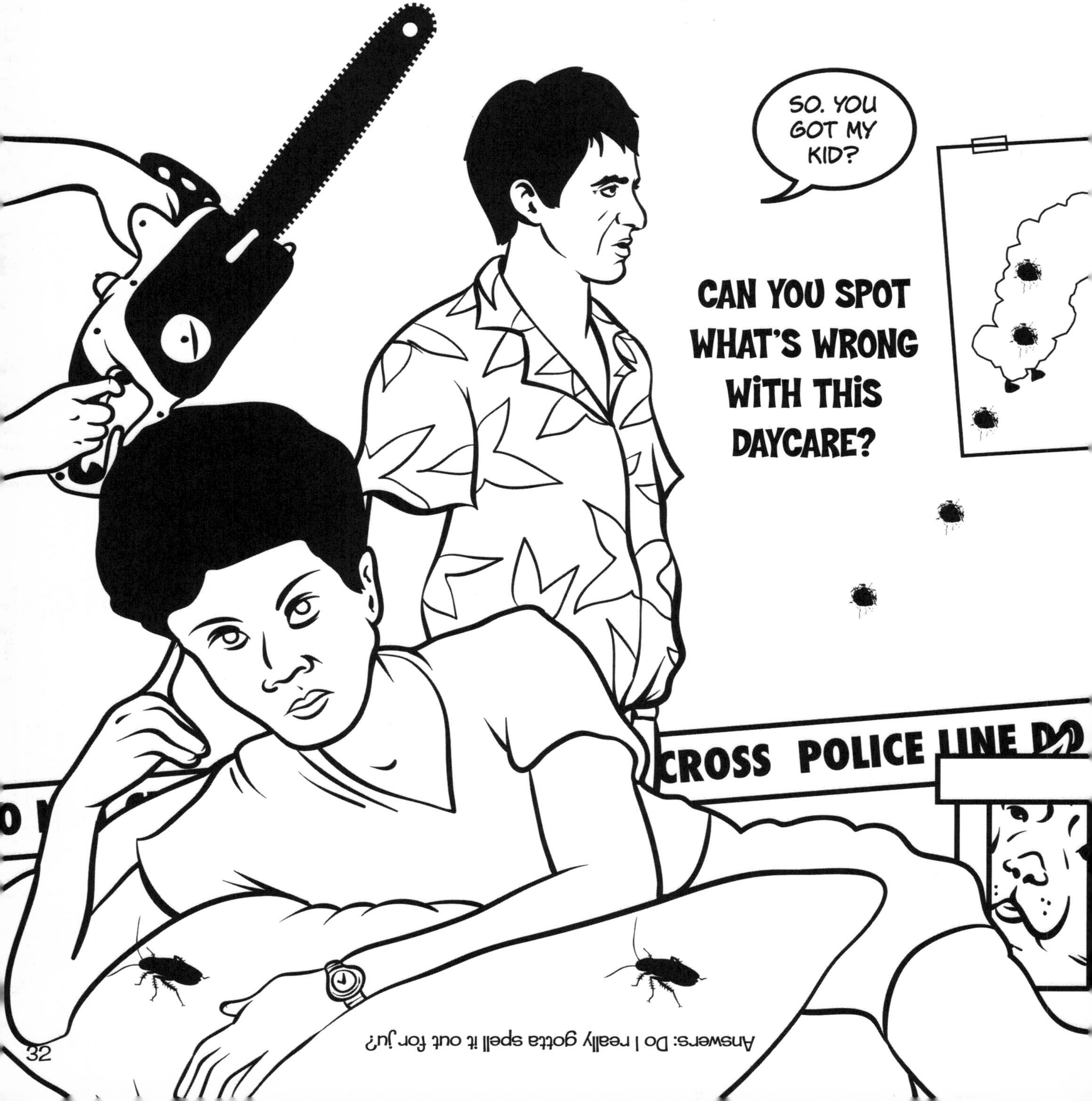

SO. YOU GOT MY KID?
CAN YOU SPOT WHAT'S WRONG WITH THIS DAYCARE?
CROSS POLICE LINE DO

Answers: Do I really gotta spell it out for ju?

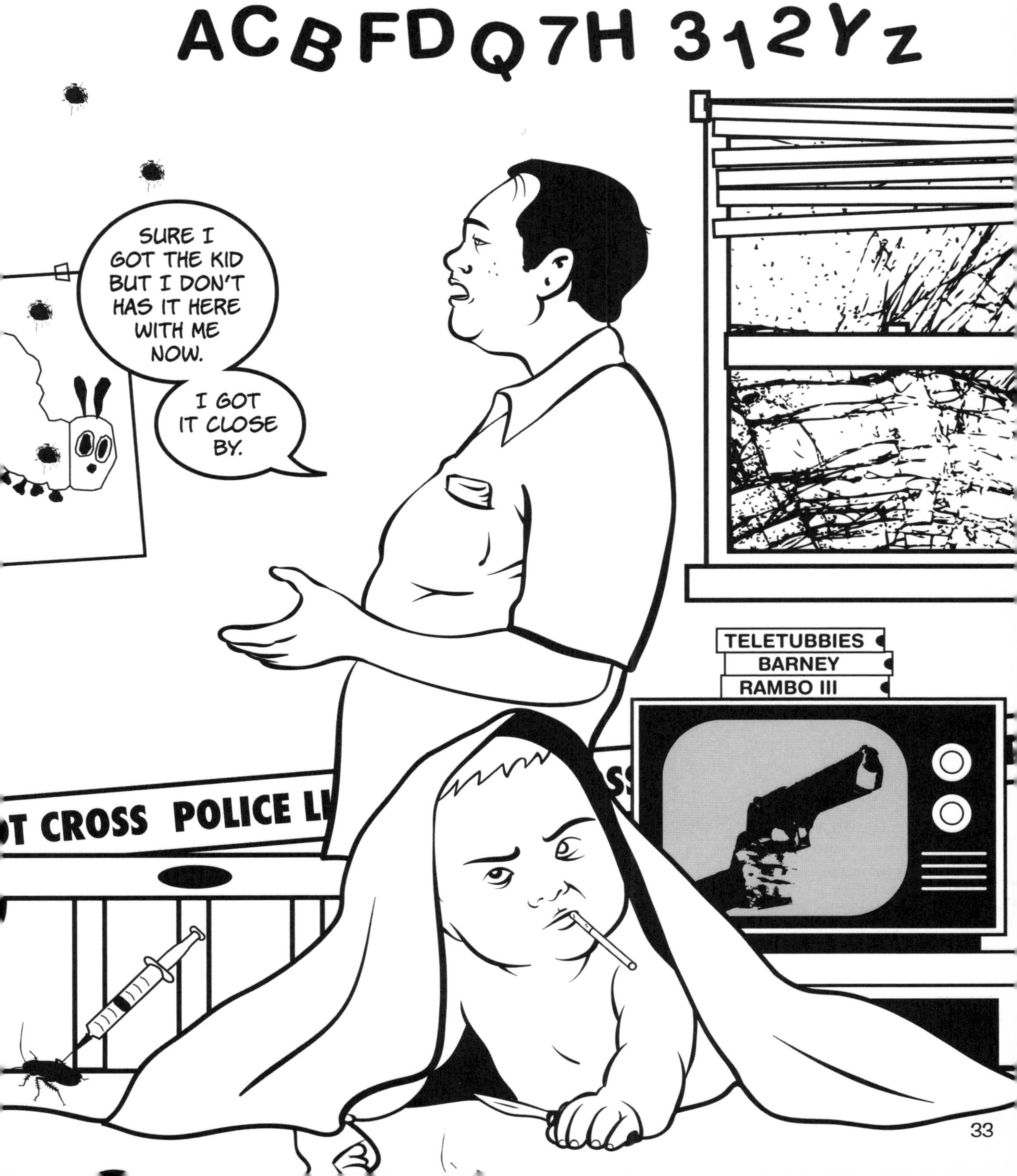
ACBFDQ7H 312Yz
SURE I GOT THE KID BUT I DON'T HAS IT HERE WITH ME NOW.
I GOT IT CLOSE BY.
TELETUBBIES
BARNEY
RAMBO III
OT CROSS POLICE LI

APPLICANT FOR DESTRUCTION

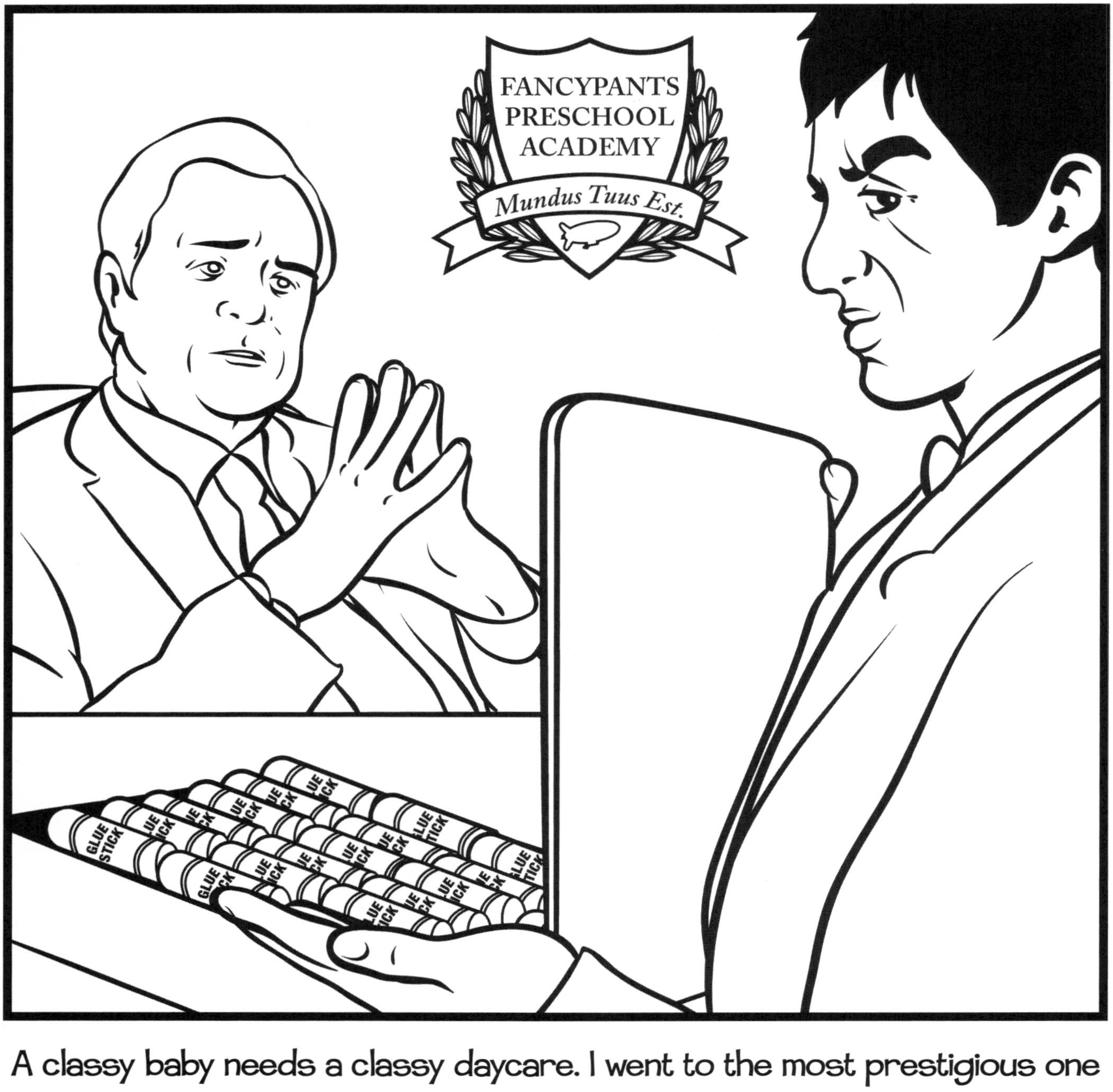
FANCYPANTS
PRESCHOOL
ACADEMY
Mundus Tuus Est.
GLUE STICK

A classy baby needs a classy daycare. I went to the most prestigious one I could find and tried to bribe my way in. But this place is way too classy for that sort of thing, so it looks like I'm gonna have to do this by the book. The Tony Montana book, that is. Written by Tony Montana. (It's <u>this</u> book!)

DAD LIBS

I always tell the truth. Even when I lie on preschool applications.

HELP TONY BULLSHIT HIS WAY INTO A GOOD DAYCARE!

FANCYPANTS PRESCHOOL ACADEMY
Mundus Tuus Est.

ENROLLMENT APPLICATION

CHILD NAME: _____

SPECIAL TALENTS: _____

INSTRUMENTS PLAYED:

CURRENT BELT IN KARATE:

_____

MILE TIME:

LANGUAGES SPOKEN:

_____

CUTENESS:
(ON A SCALE OF 1-10)

| 1 | 2 | 3 | 4 | 5 | 6 | 7 | 8 | 9 | 10 |

FAVORITE MICHAEL CHABON BOOK:

_____

BSAT SCORE
(BABY SAT):

_____

THE COKE'S ON JU

Ju never gonna believe this, but apparently all the parents who were on the waiting list ahead of us were arrested for cocaine posession. What a crazy coincidence that I don't know nothing about!

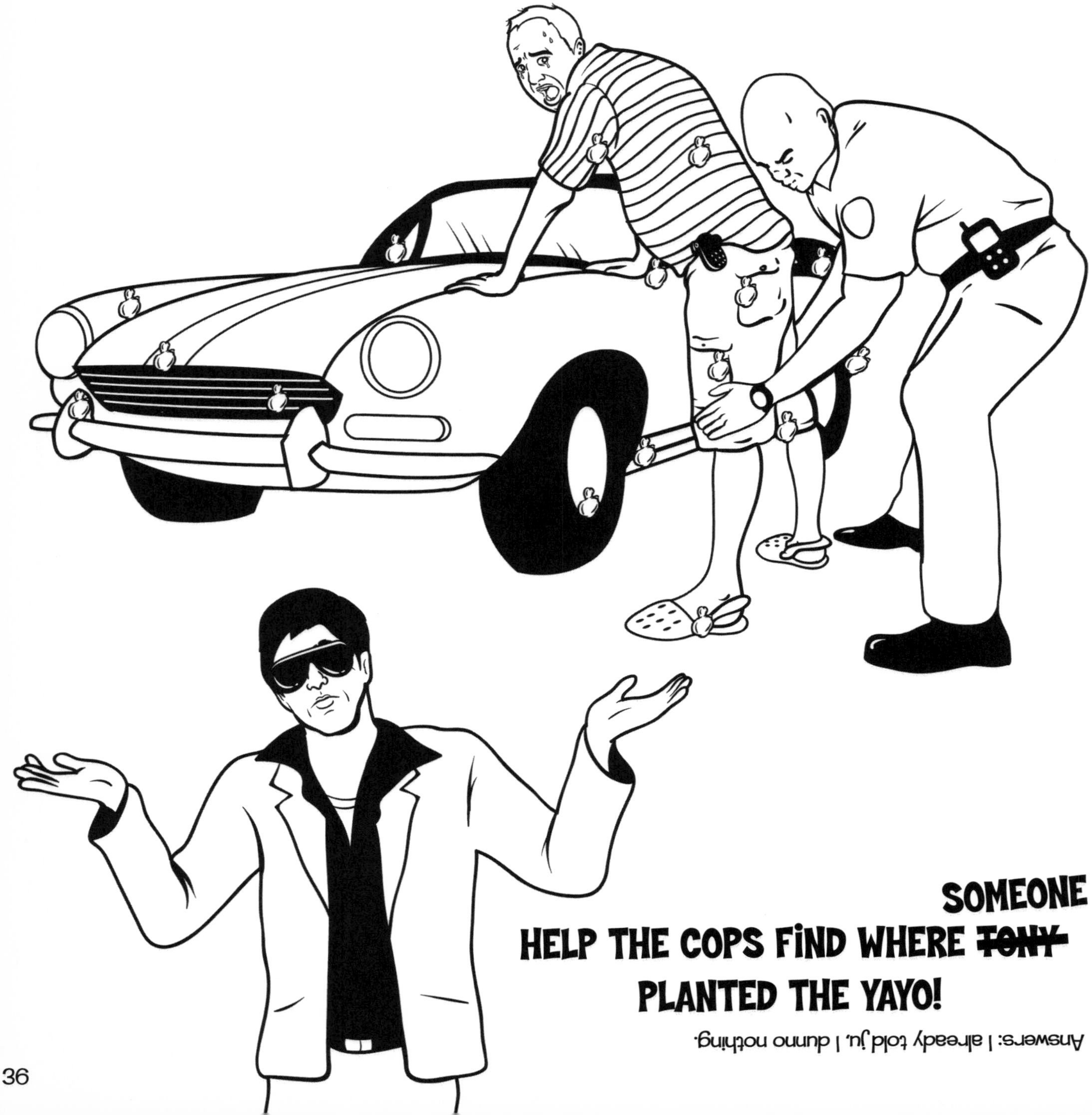

HELP THE COPS FIND WHERE ~~TONY~~ SOMEONE PLANTED THE YAYO!

Answers: I already told ju. I dunno nothing.

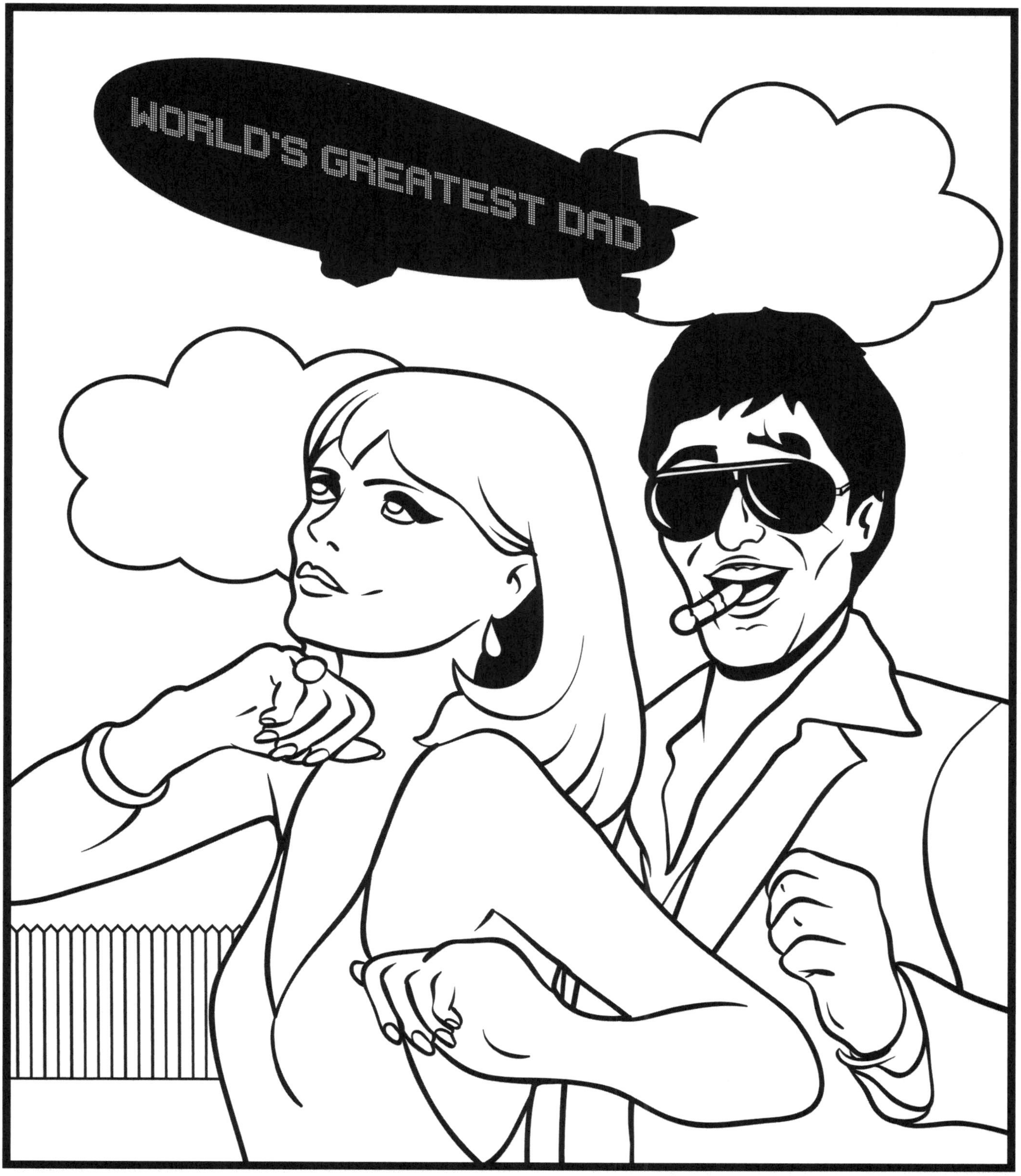
WORLD'S GREATEST DAD

I just got my kid into the top-rated daycare in town. Even better, I got him into bed tonight before 8:30. Damn, it feels good to be a gangster.

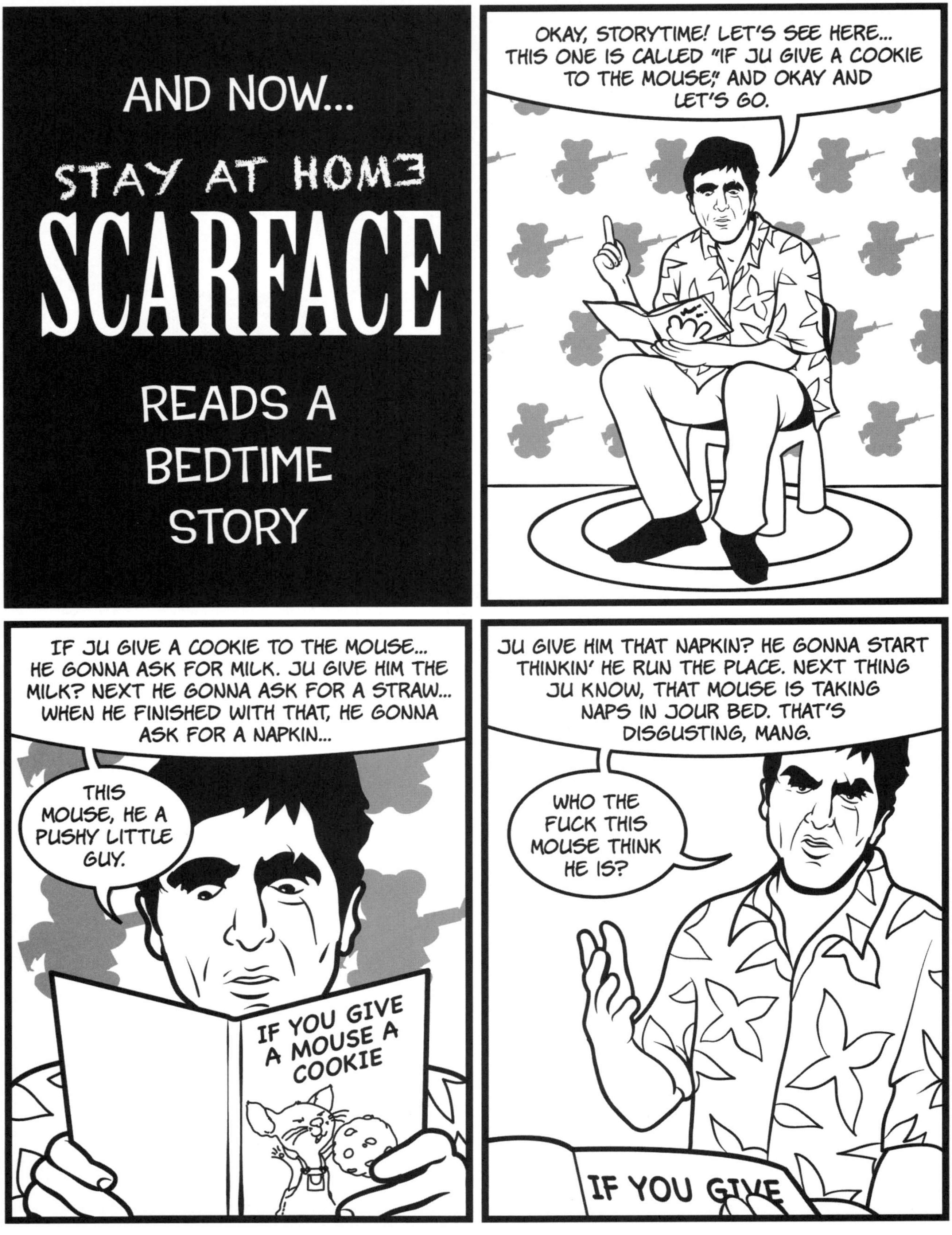
AND NOW...
STAY AT HOM3
SCARFACE
READS A BEDTIME STORY
OKAY, STORYTIME! LET'S SEE HERE... THIS ONE IS CALLED "IF JU GIVE A COOKIE TO THE MOUSE," AND OKAY AND LET'S GO.
IF JU GIVE A COOKIE TO THE MOUSE... HE GONNA ASK FOR MILK. JU GIVE HIM THE MILK? NEXT HE GONNA ASK FOR A STRAW... WHEN HE FINISHED WITH THAT, HE GONNA ASK FOR A NAPKIN...
THIS MOUSE, HE A PUSHY LITTLE GUY.
IF YOU GIVE A MOUSE A COOKIE
JU GIVE HIM THAT NAPKIN? HE GONNA START THINKIN' HE RUN THE PLACE. NEXT THING JU KNOW, THAT MOUSE IS TAKING NAPS IN JOUR BED. THAT'S DISGUSTING, MANG.
WHO THE FUCK THIS MOUSE THINK HE IS?
IF YOU GIVE

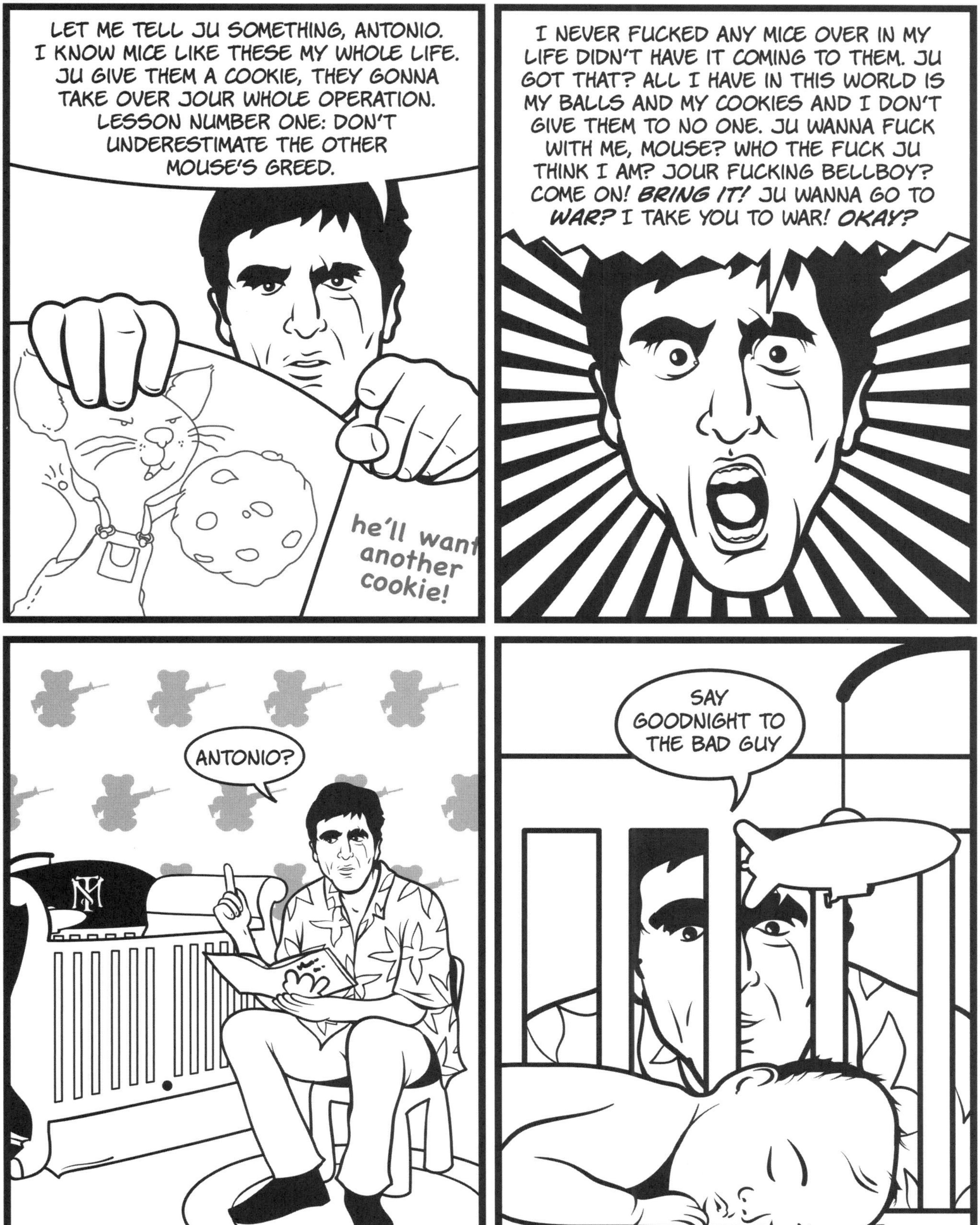
LET ME TELL JU SOMETHING, ANTONIO. I KNOW MICE LIKE THESE MY WHOLE LIFE. JU GIVE THEM A COOKIE, THEY GONNA TAKE OVER JOUR WHOLE OPERATION. LESSON NUMBER ONE: DON'T UNDERESTIMATE THE OTHER MOUSE'S GREED.
he'll want another cookie!
I NEVER FUCKED ANY MICE OVER IN MY LIFE DIDN'T HAVE IT COMING TO THEM. JU GOT THAT? ALL I HAVE IN THIS WORLD IS MY BALLS AND MY COOKIES AND I DON'T GIVE THEM TO NO ONE. JU WANNA FUCK WITH ME, MOUSE? WHO THE FUCK JU THINK I AM? JOUR FUCKING BELLBOY? COME ON! BRING IT! JU WANNA GO TO WAR? I TAKE YOU TO WAR! OKAY?
ANTONIO?
SAY GOODNIGHT TO THE BAD GUY

TONY TAKES A SELFiE

It's Little Antonio's first day of daycare. I'm gonna take a picture to remember this day forever. Aww, look at that. He has my scowl.

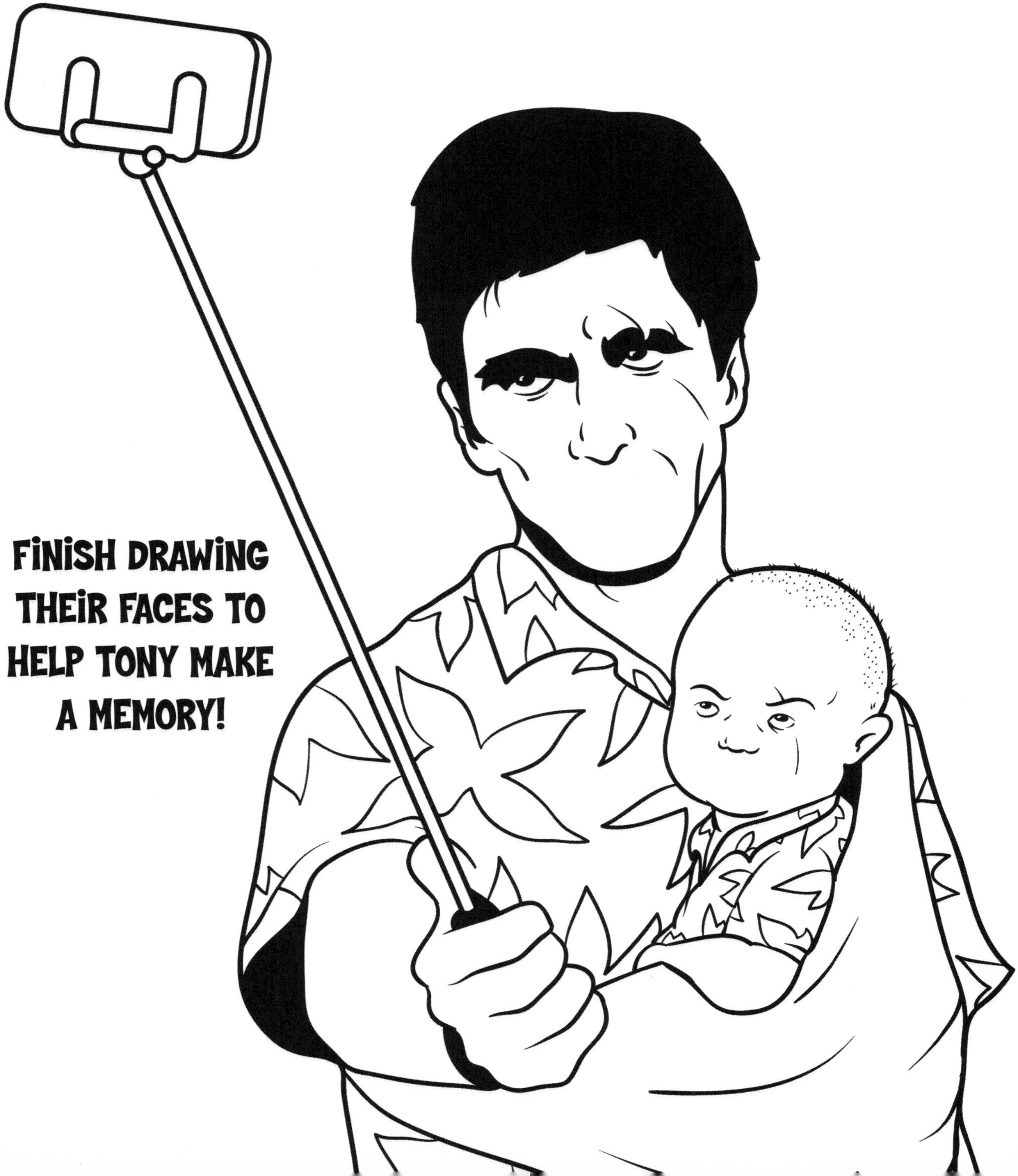

FiNiSH DRAWiNG THEiR FACES TO HELP TONY MAKE A MEMORY!

THE PARENT TRAP

Ugh, other parents. I'd rather be tied up in a motel shower with a chainsaw to my throat than spend five minutes with these guys.

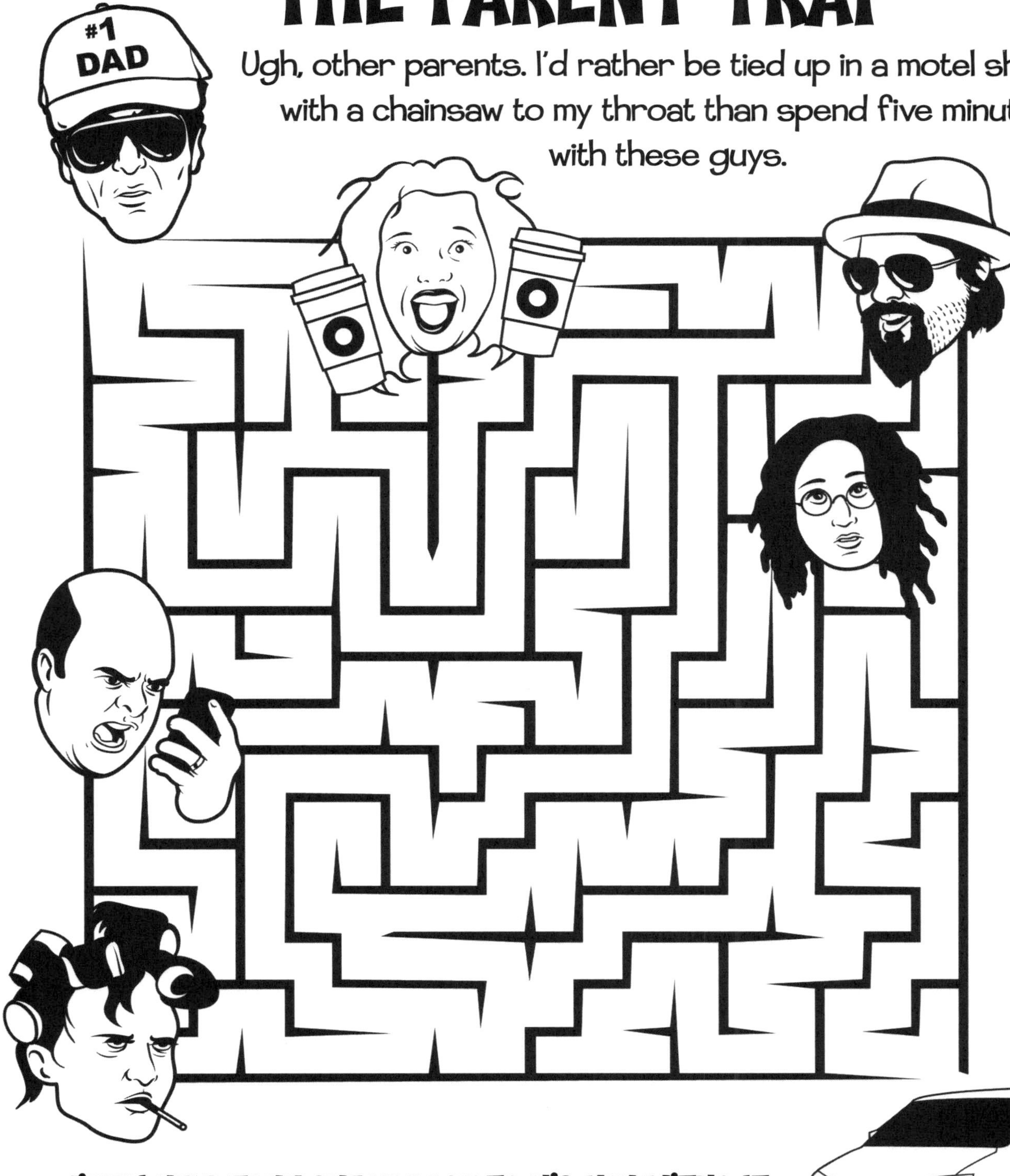
#1
DAD

YIKES! HELP TONY SNEAK BACK TO HIS VAN WITHOUT RUNNING INTO COFFEE MOM, COOL DAD, GRANOLA MOM, RAGE DAD, OR DEVIL MOM.

EVERY DAD HAS HIS DAY

Now that the little rugrat is in school all day, I can finally get some rest and relaxation! This is paradise, I'm telling ju.

BEFORE DAYCARE

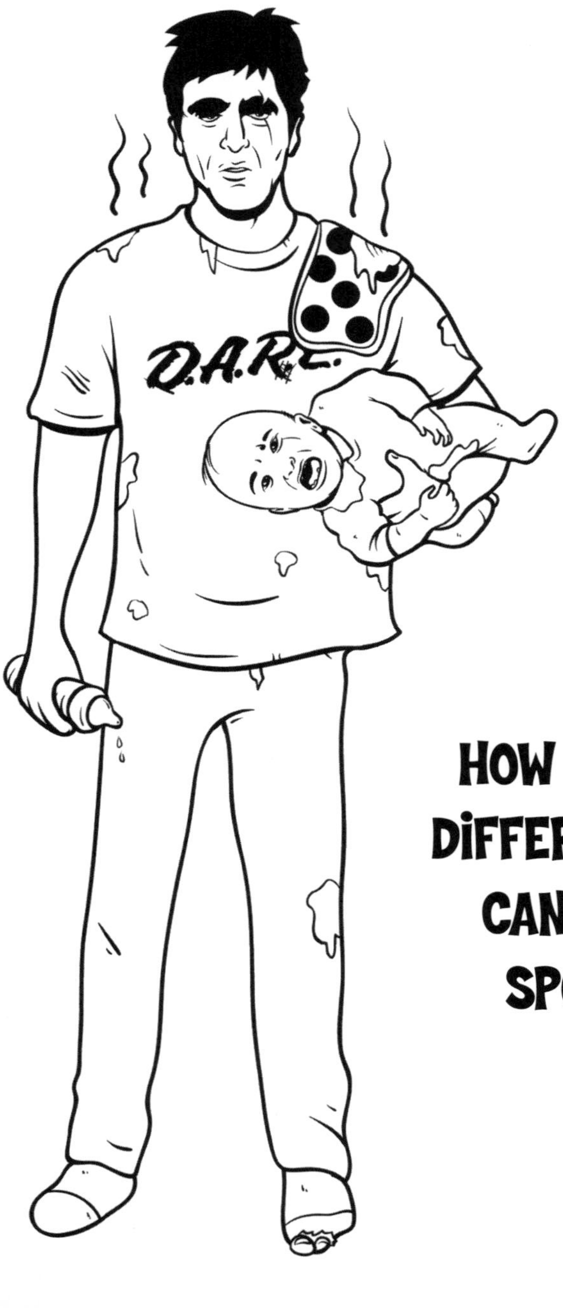
D.A.R.E.

AFTER DAYCARE

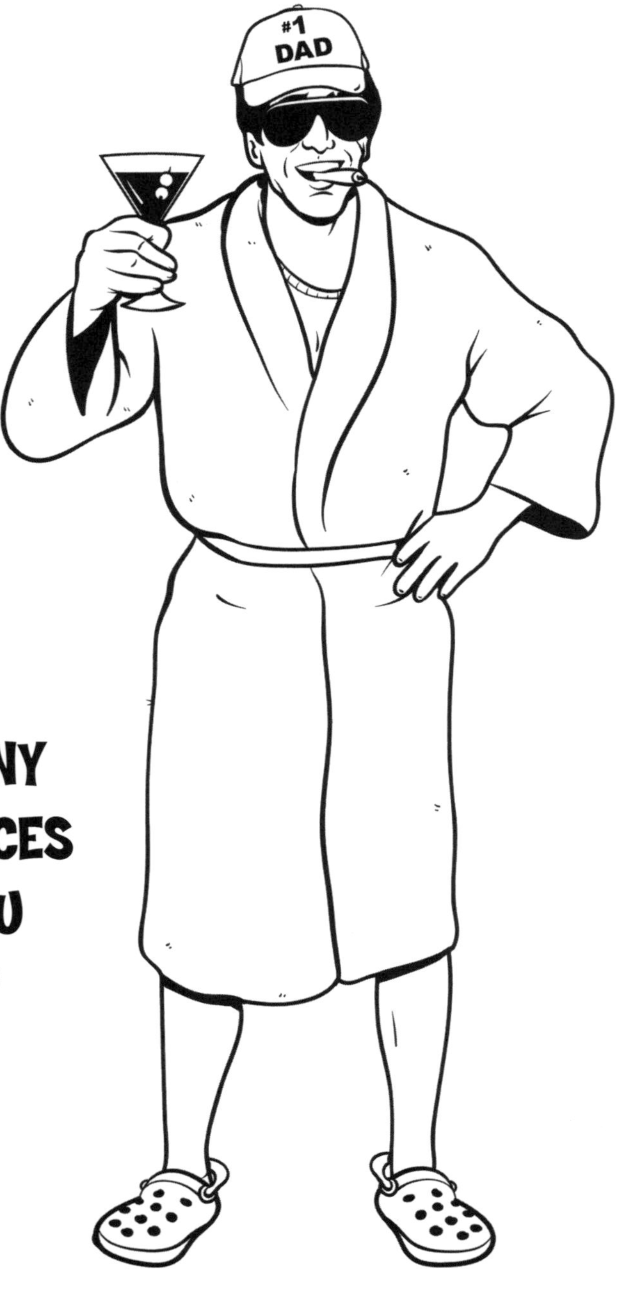
#1
DAD

HOW MANY DIFFERENCES CAN YOU SPOT?

Answers: I dunno, try C again.

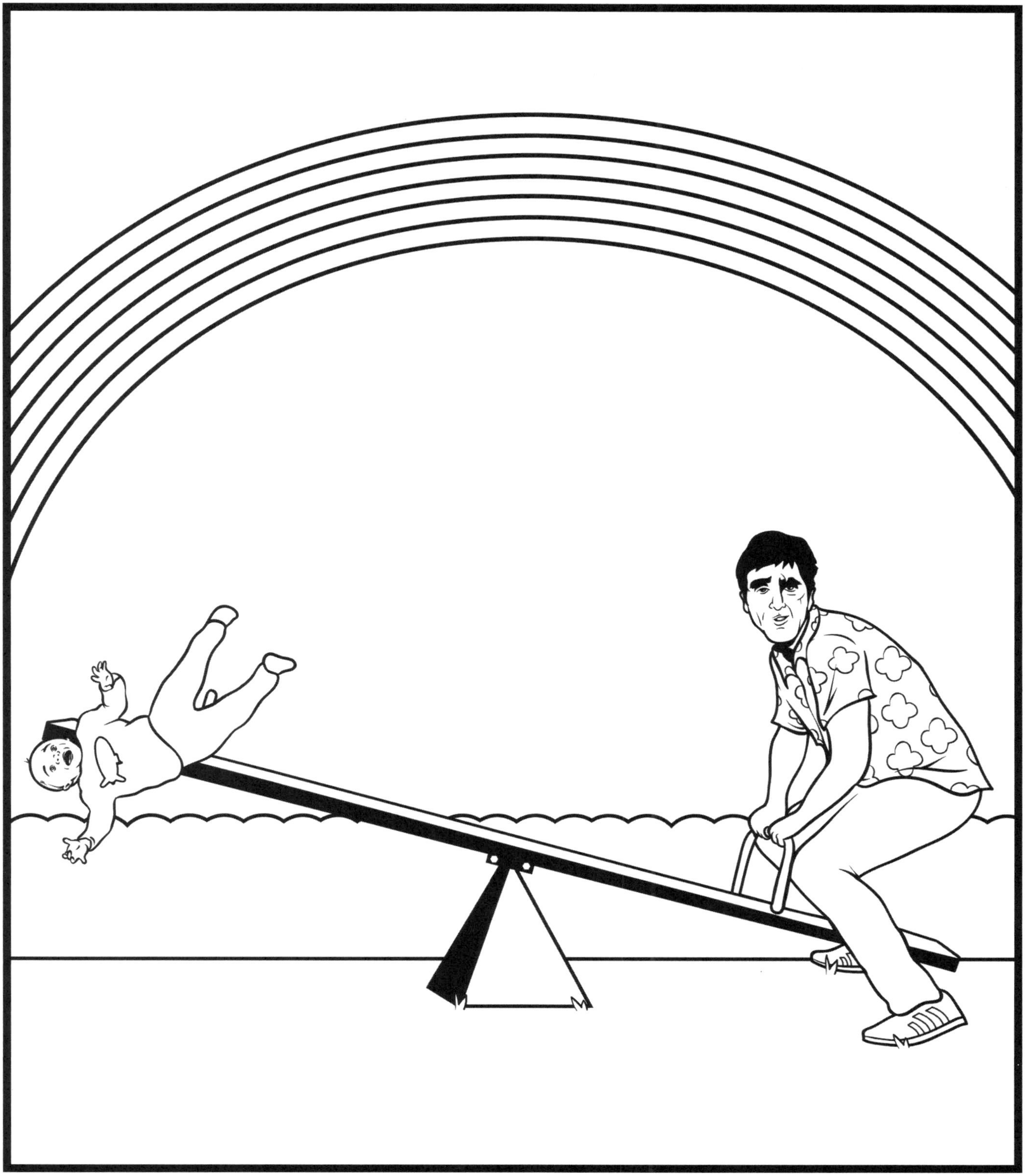

Parenting has its ups and downs, but
I think I'm finally starting to get the hang of it, mang.

TONY MAKES AN ENEMY

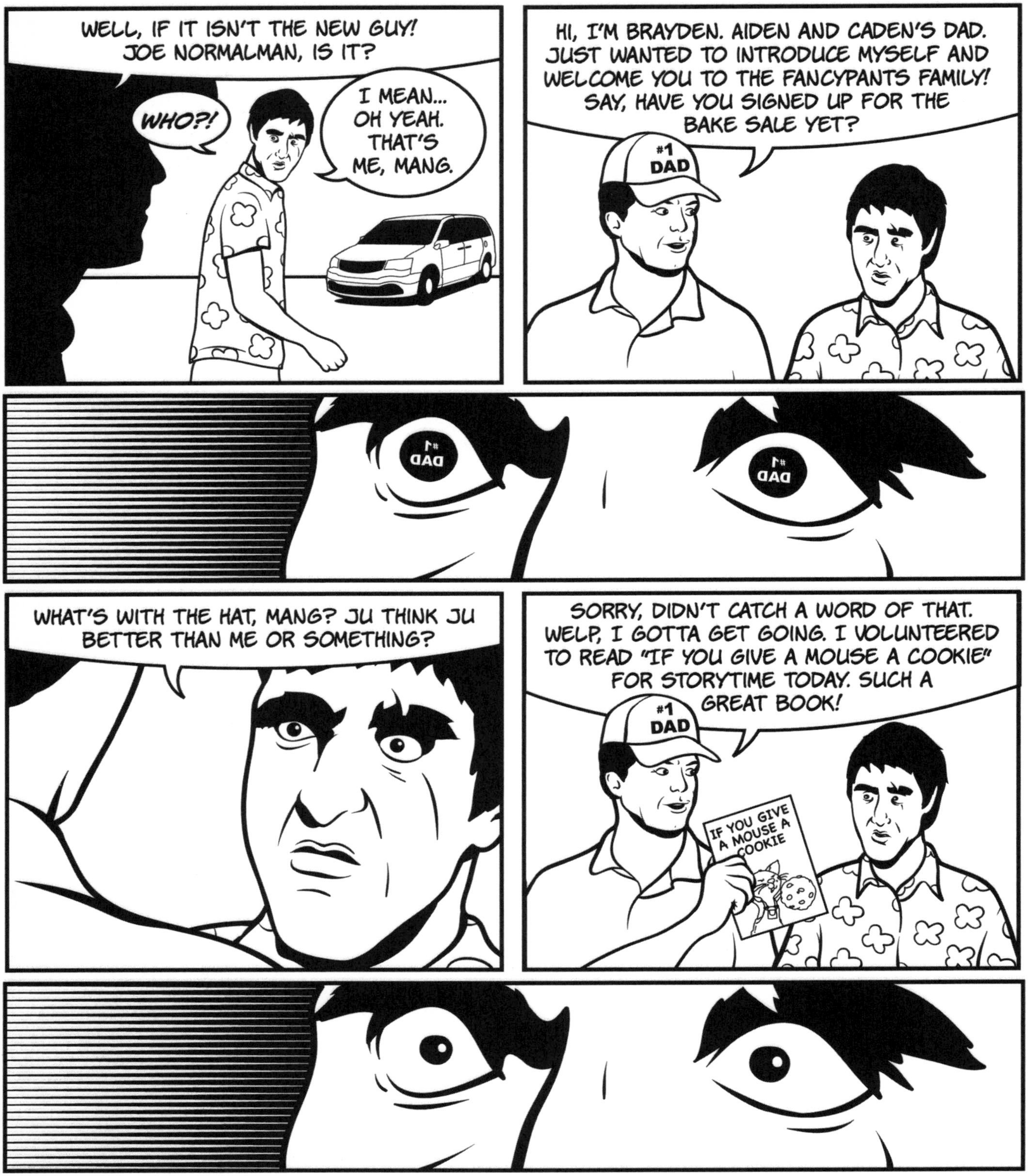
WELL, IF IT ISN'T THE NEW GUY! JOE NORMALMAN, IS IT?
WHO?!
I MEAN... OH YEAH. THAT'S ME, MANG.
HI, I'M BRAYDEN. AIDEN AND CADEN'S DAD. JUST WANTED TO INTRODUCE MYSELF AND WELCOME YOU TO THE FANCYPANTS FAMILY! SAY, HAVE YOU SIGNED UP FOR THE BAKE SALE YET?
#1 DAD
WHAT'S WITH THE HAT, MANG? JU THINK JU BETTER THAN ME OR SOMETHING?
SORRY, DIDN'T CATCH A WORD OF THAT. WELP, I GOTTA GET GOING. I VOLUNTEERED TO READ "IF YOU GIVE A MOUSE A COOKIE" FOR STORYTIME TODAY. SUCH A GREAT BOOK!
#1 DAD
IF YOU GIVE A MOUSE A COOKIE

FUCKIN' WITH THE BEST

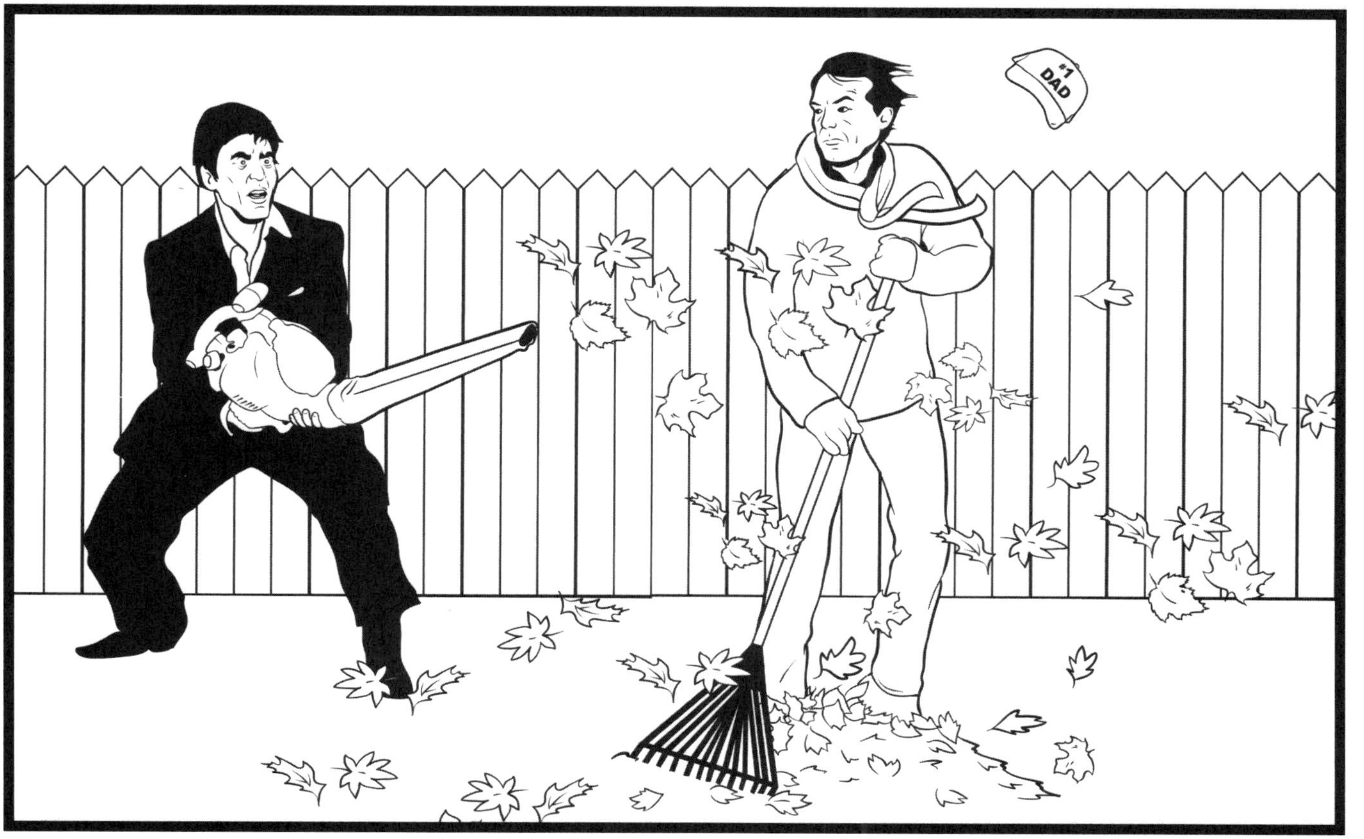
#1
DAD

I was finally gonna get what was coming to me. The daycare and everything in it. But then, in walks this fucking worm like he owns the place!

This prick thinks he's the #1 dad? Just 'cause he tells some stories to some fucking kids? Ooh, ju a big shot, huh? Reading stories to kids. How about ju read my hat, mang?

That's right. There's only one #1 Dad in this town. And his name rhymes with Mony Tontana. (It's me, Tony Montana.)

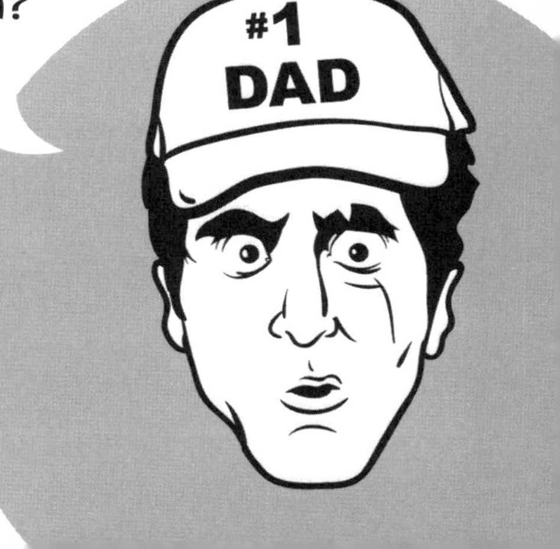
#1
DAD

TONY HAS A BEEF

I grill a steak for fun... but for this guy? I'm gonna cook it up real nice.

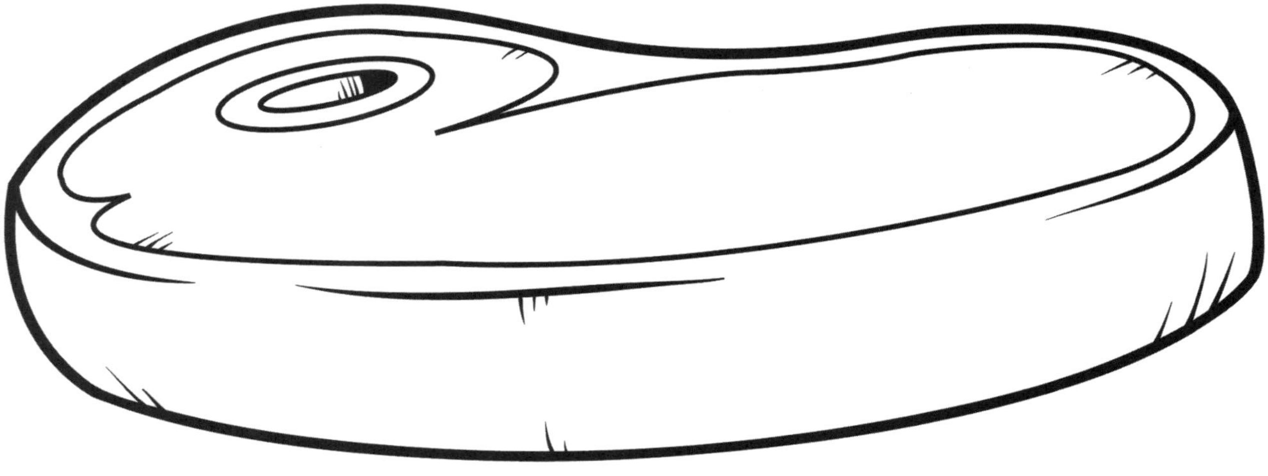

COLOR THE STEAK TO PERFECTION TO SHOW HIM WHO'S BOSS

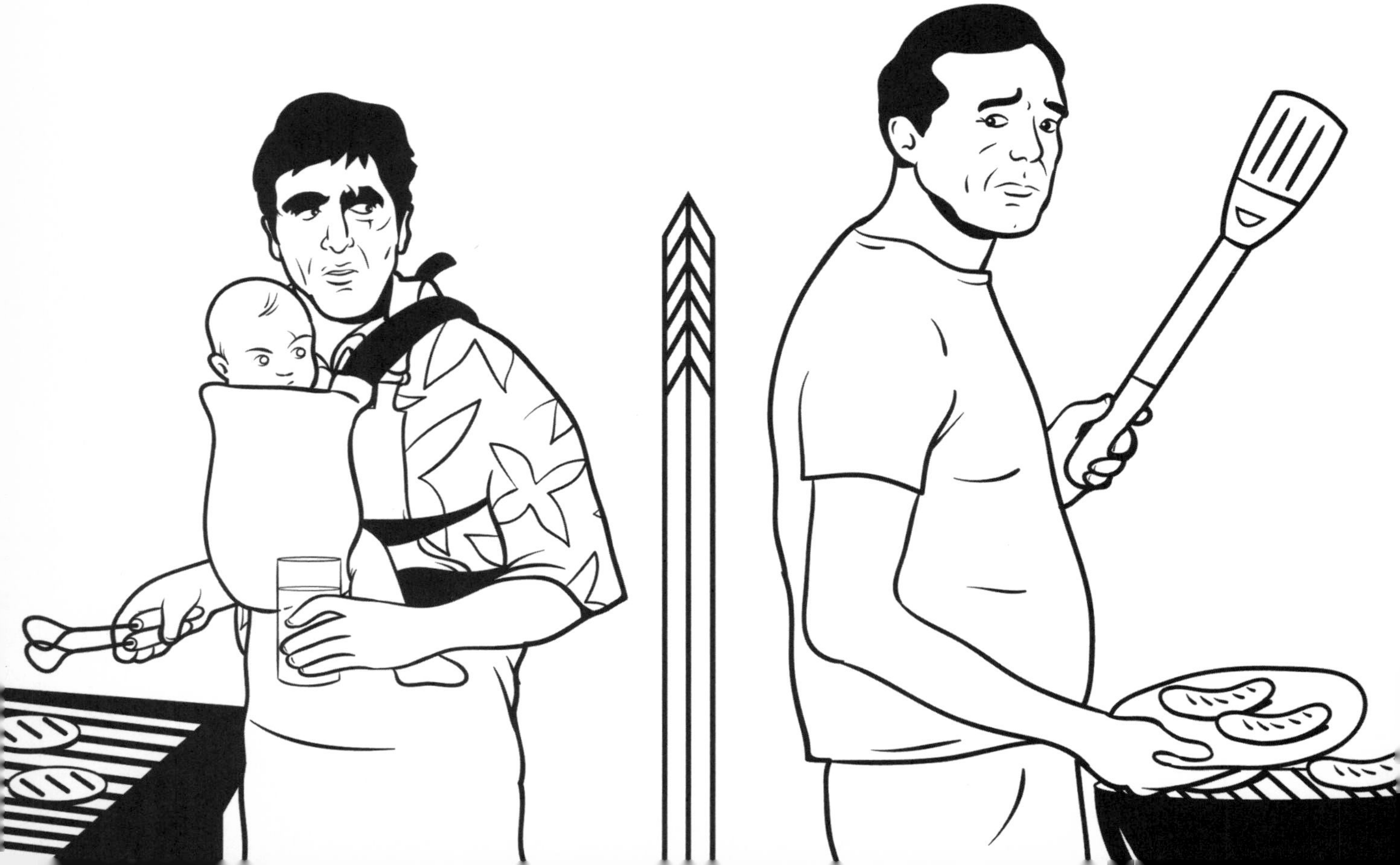

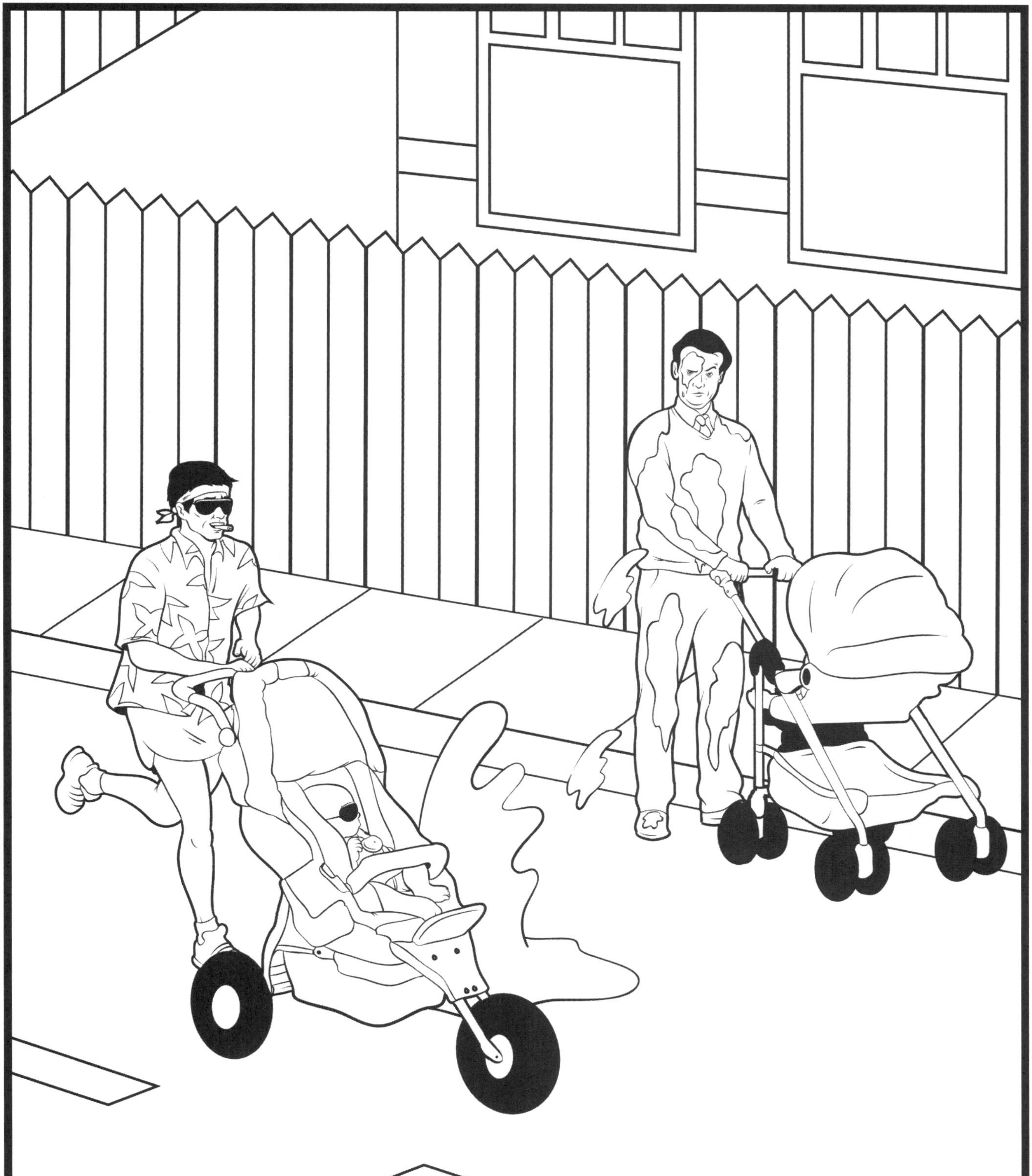

TONY MONTANA RUNS THESE STREETS, JU HEAR ME?!

MOW PROBLEMS

This guy still ain't getting it. So I'm gonna send him a little message right where it hurts – in his lawn.

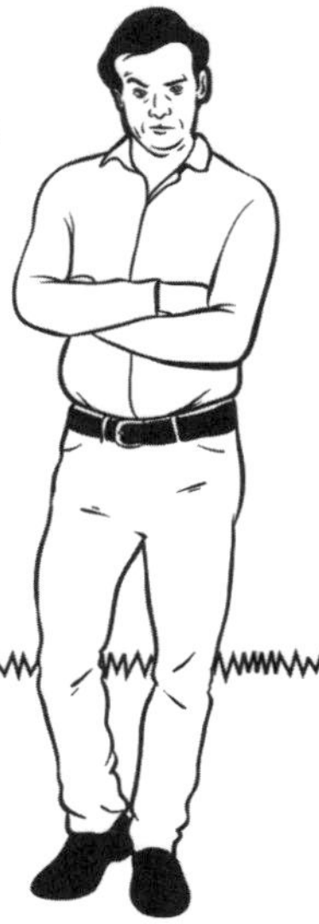

COLOR BY NUMBERS TO REVEAL TONY'S MESSAGE

1 - GREEN 2 -BROWN

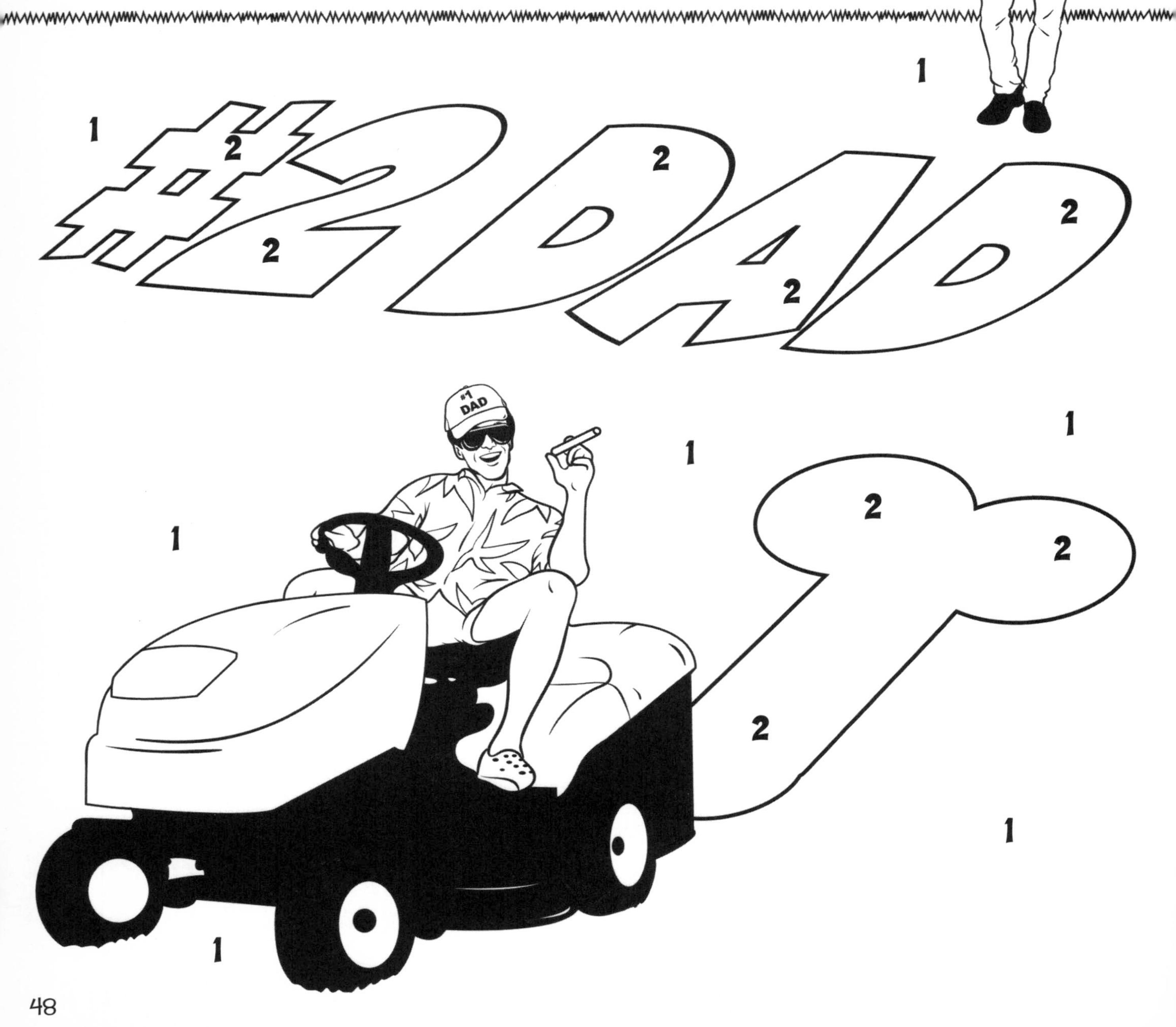
1
1
2
#2 DAD
2
2
2
2
#1 DAD
1
1
1
2
2
2
1
1

NOW JOU'RE COOKIN'

The school bake sale is coming up and I gotta show all these other parents how it's done. There's just one tiny problem: I don't know how to read these recipes! What the fuck is a "teaspoon," mang?

TONY'S LEMON SQUARES		TONY'S LEMON SQUARES
1 cup flour	=	___ kilos flour
1/2 cup butter, softened		___ kilos butter, softened
1/4 cup powdered sugar		___ kilos powdered sugar
1 cup granulated sugar		___ kilos granulated sugar
2 teaspoons grated lemon peel		___ kilos grated lemon peel
2 tablespoons lemon juice		___ kilos lemon juice
1/2 teaspoon baking powder		___ kilos baking powder
1/4 teaspoon salt		___ kilos teaspoon salt
2 eggs		___ kilos eggs
powdered sugar to taste		powdered sugar to taste

HELP TONY CONVERT ALL THE UNITS TO KILOS SO HE'LL KNOW HOW TO MEASURE THEM!

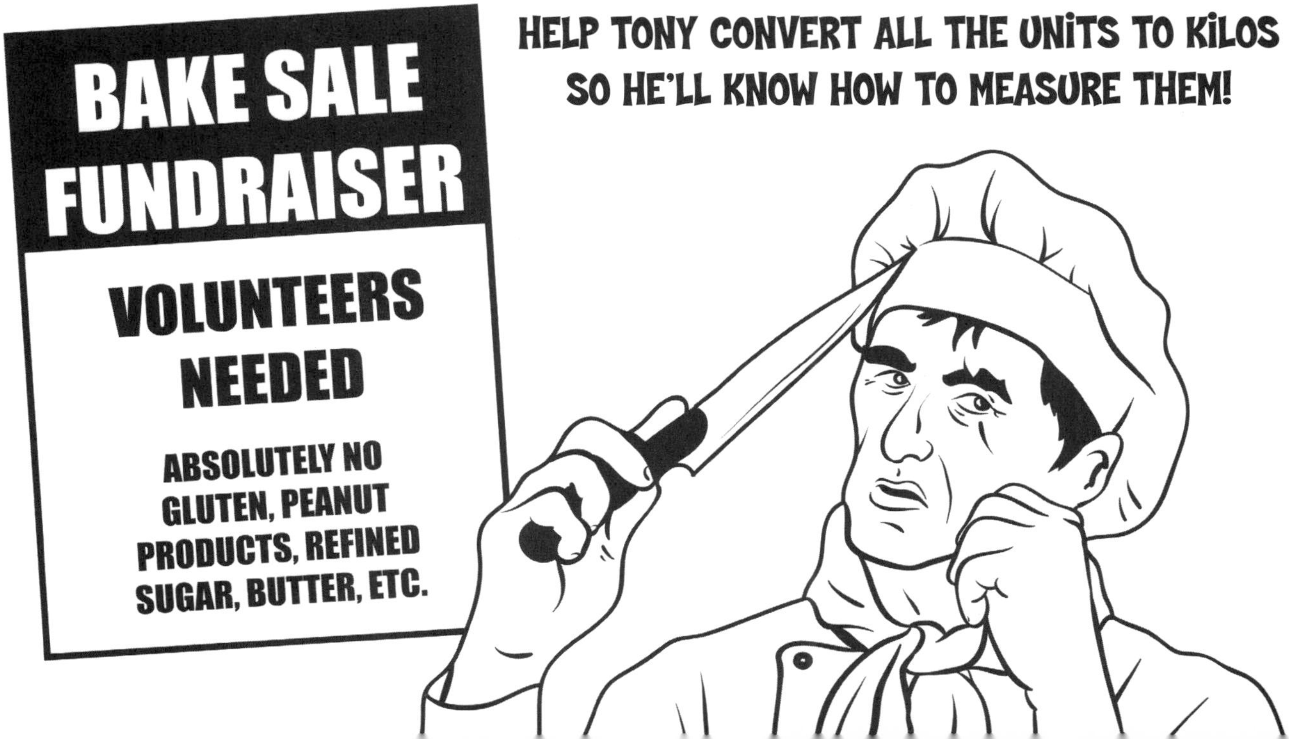
BAKE SALE FUNDRAISER
VOLUNTEERS NEEDED
ABSOLUTELY NO GLUTEN, PEANUT PRODUCTS, REFINED SUGAR, BUTTER, ETC.

Answers: Tony Montana don't answer to nobody, mang.

TONY HAS A BAKE SALE

It's time to put my operation together.

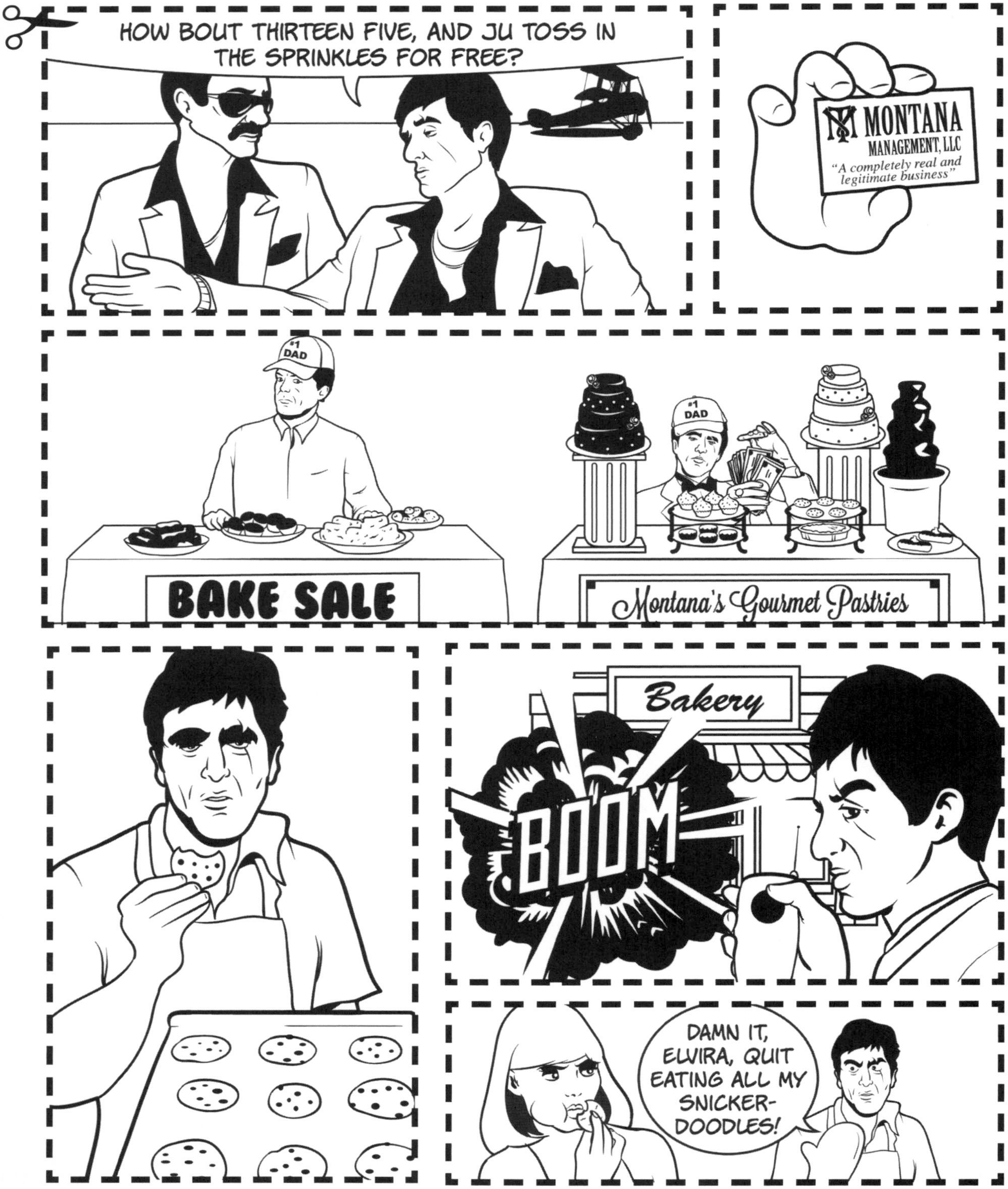
HOW BOUT THIRTEEN FIVE, AND JU TOSS IN THE SPRINKLES FOR FREE?
MONTANA MANAGEMENT, LLC
"A completely real and legitimate business"
#1 DAD
BAKE SALE
#1 DAD
Montana's Gourmet Pastries
Bakery
BOOM
DAMN IT, ELVIRA, QUIT EATING ALL MY SNICKER-DOODLES!

CUT OUT THE PANELS AND ARRANGE THEM IN THE RIGHT ORDER TO TAKE OVER THE BAKE SALE GAME!

Set up a dummy corporation for tax purposes.

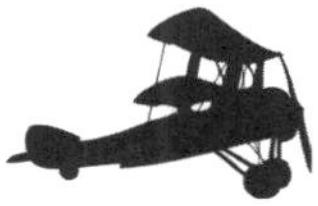

Meet with Colombian sugar cartel to negotiate a lower price point for wholesale cookie dough distribution.

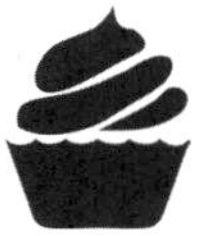

Learn to bake.

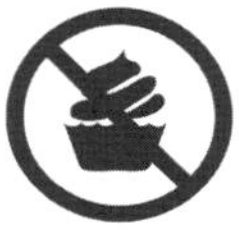

Don't get high on your own supply.

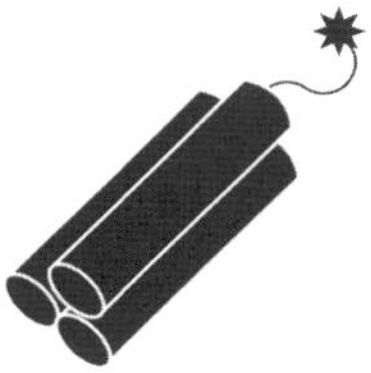

Eliminate the competition.

$$$

Set up shop and rake in the cash.

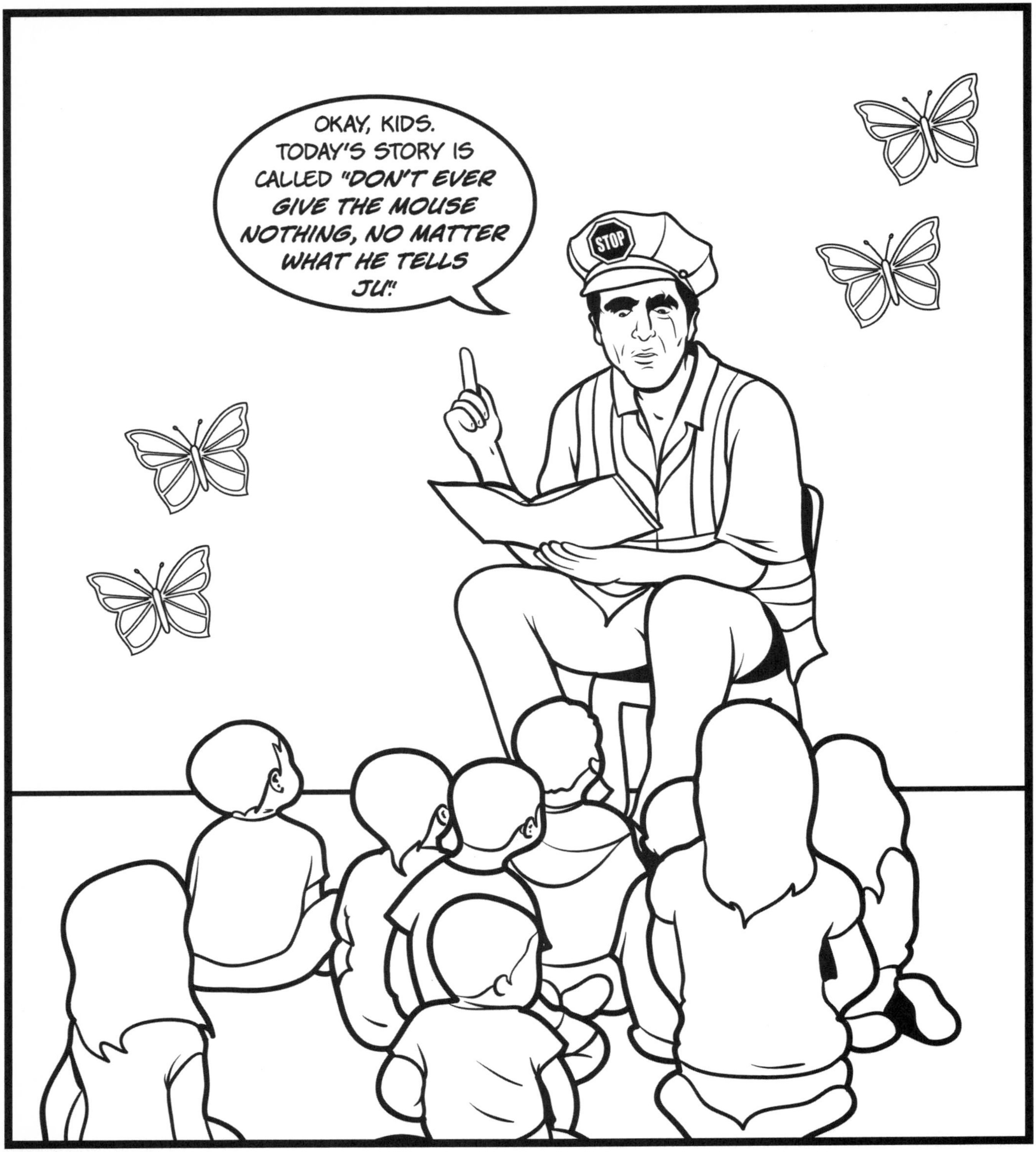
OKAY, KIDS. TODAY'S STORY IS CALLED "DON'T EVER GIVE THE MOUSE NOTHING, NO MATTER WHAT HE TELLS JU."
STOP

In this daycare, ju gotta work the bake sale first. Then when ju work the bake sale, ju get the crossing guard duty. Then when ju get the crossing guard duty, ju get to do story time.

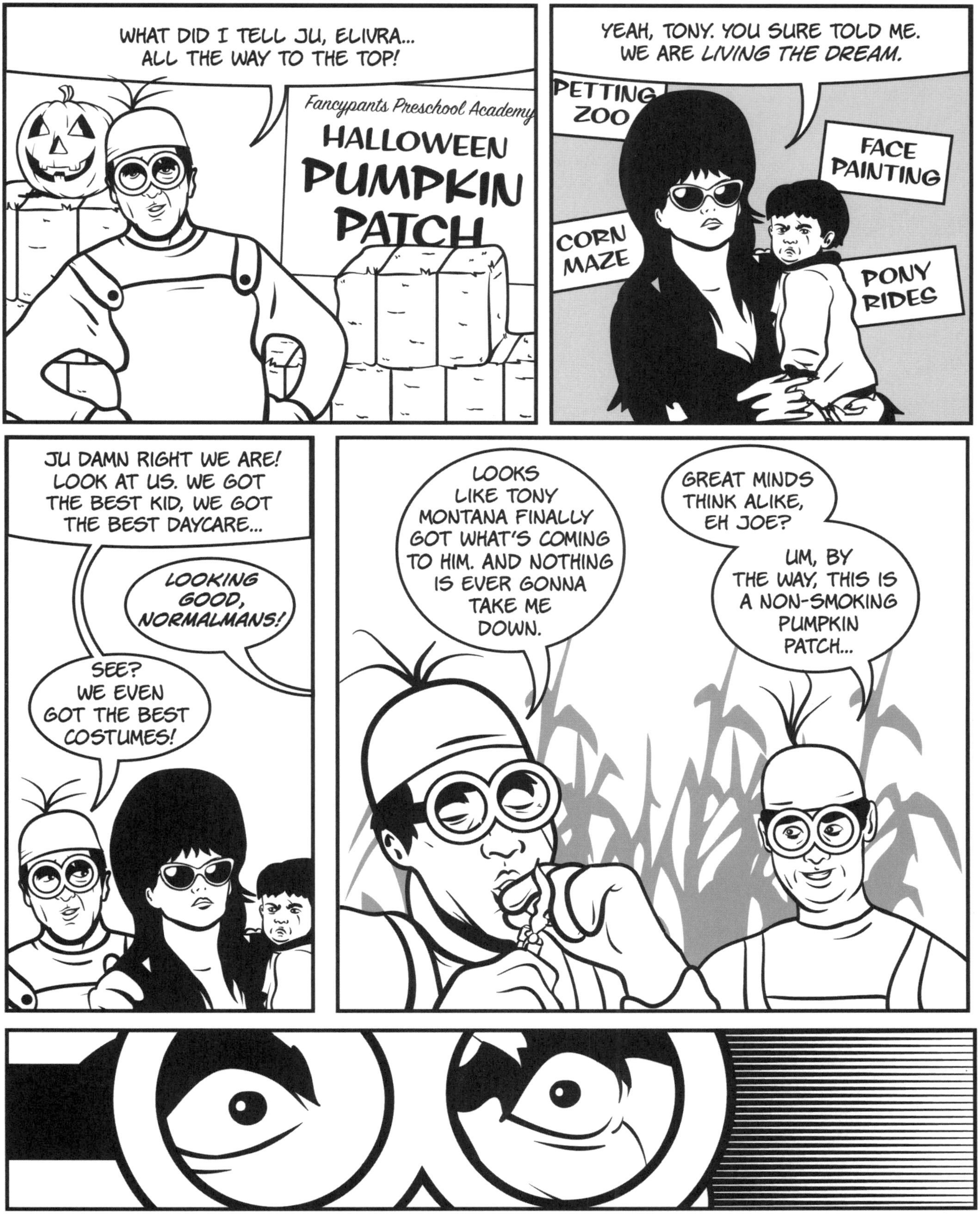
WHAT DID I TELL JU, ELIVRA... ALL THE WAY TO THE TOP!
Fancypants Preschool Academy
HALLOWEEN PUMPKIN PATCH
YEAH, TONY. YOU SURE TOLD ME. WE ARE LIVING THE DREAM.
PETTING ZOO
FACE PAINTING
CORN MAZE
PONY RIDES
JU DAMN RIGHT WE ARE! LOOK AT US. WE GOT THE BEST KID, WE GOT THE BEST DAYCARE...
LOOKING GOOD, NORMALMANS!
SEE? WE EVEN GOT THE BEST COSTUMES!
LOOKS LIKE TONY MONTANA FINALLY GOT WHAT'S COMING TO HIM. AND NOTHING IS EVER GONNA TAKE ME DOWN.
GREAT MINDS THINK ALIKE, EH JOE?
UM, BY THE WAY, THIS IS A NON-SMOKING PUMPKIN PATCH...

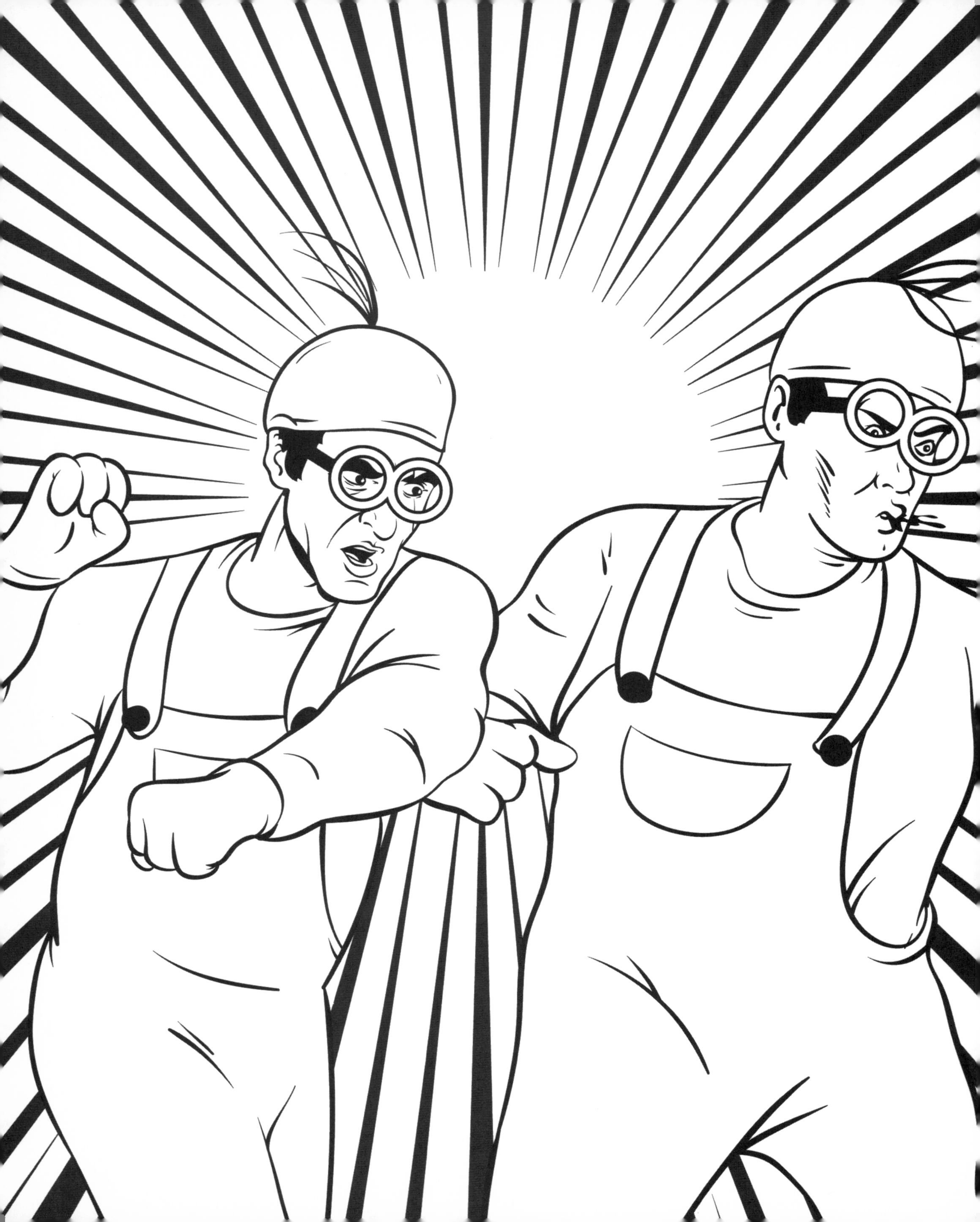

TONY GETS EXPELLED

Ju know what? Fuck ju! How about that?

CONNECT THE DOTS TO SEE HOW TONY REALLY FEELS ABOUT IT.

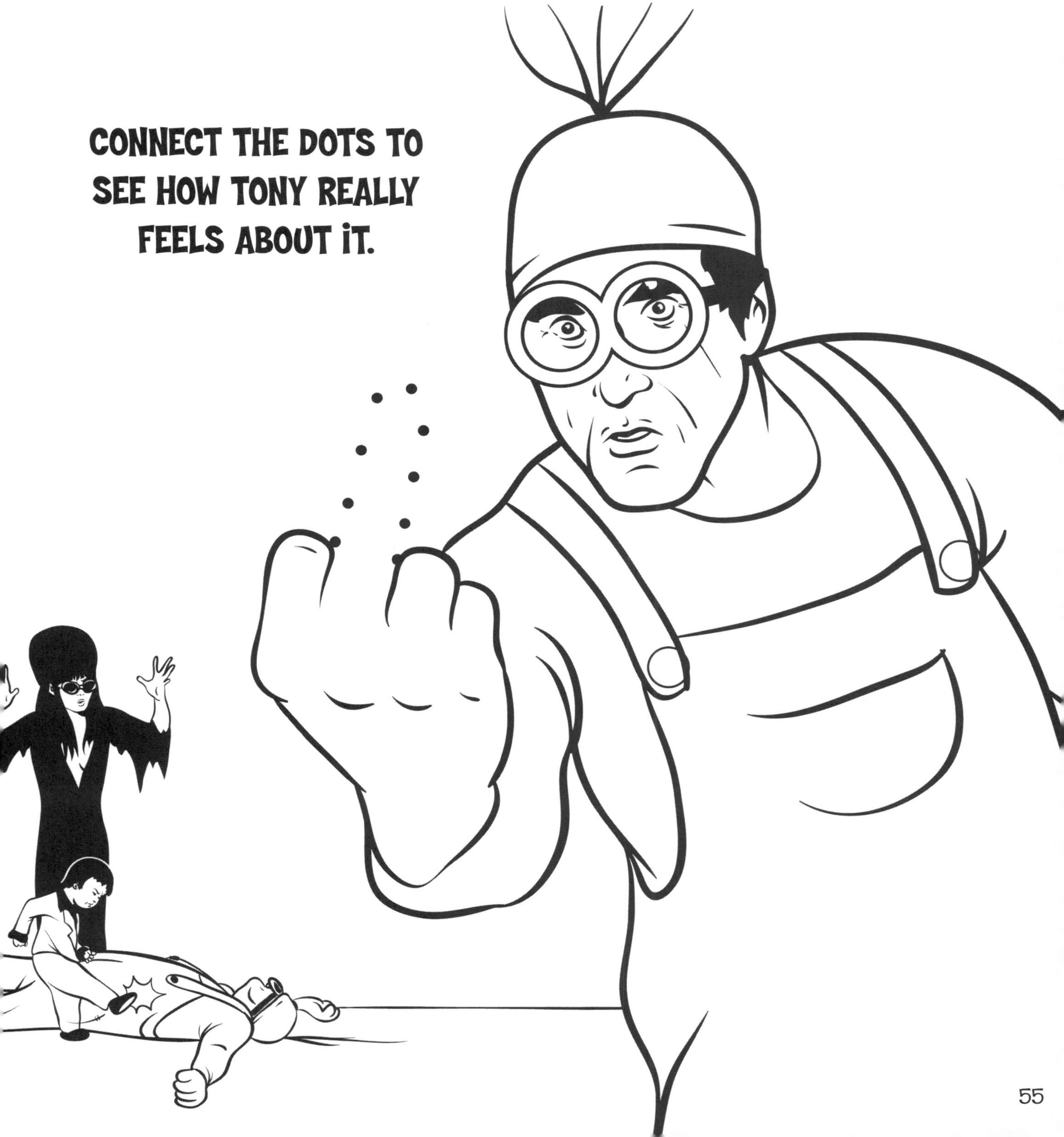

JU WiN SOME, JU LOSE SOME

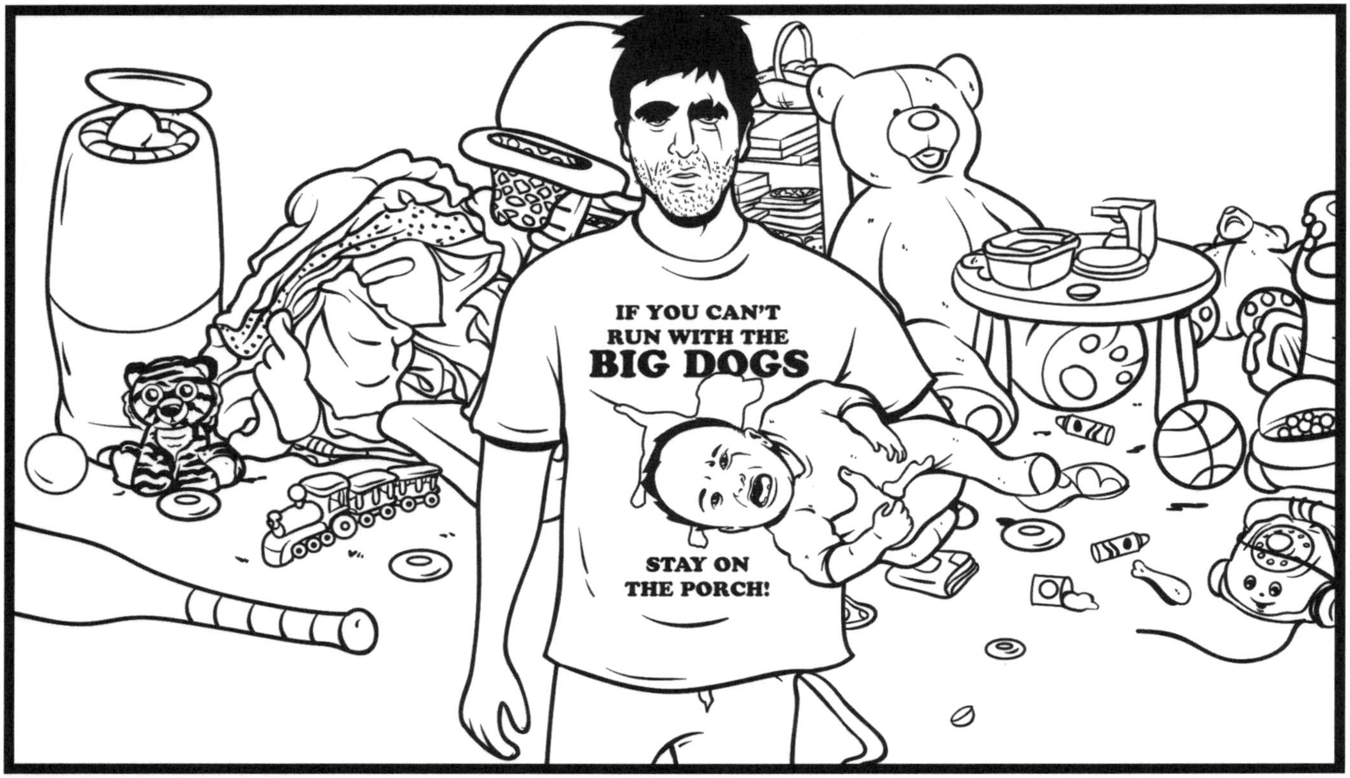
IF YOU CAN'T
RUN WITH THE
BIG DOGS
STAY ON
THE PORCH!

Now that we been blacklisted from every childcare facility in the county, guess I'm gonna be homeschooling Little Antonio for a while.

That's okay. To tell ju the truth, I was getting kind of tired of just sitting in the hot tub all day, watching old gangster movies, and being able to hear myself think. Things are much more interesting with Little Antonio scampering around all over the place! Like the other day, when he took a shit all over the model train set I had just spent 3 months working on. I tell ju, every day is an adventure with that kid around!

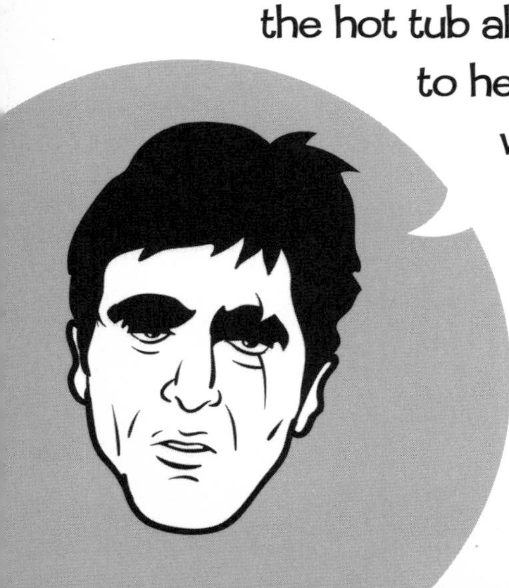

I could sure use a quaalude right about now.

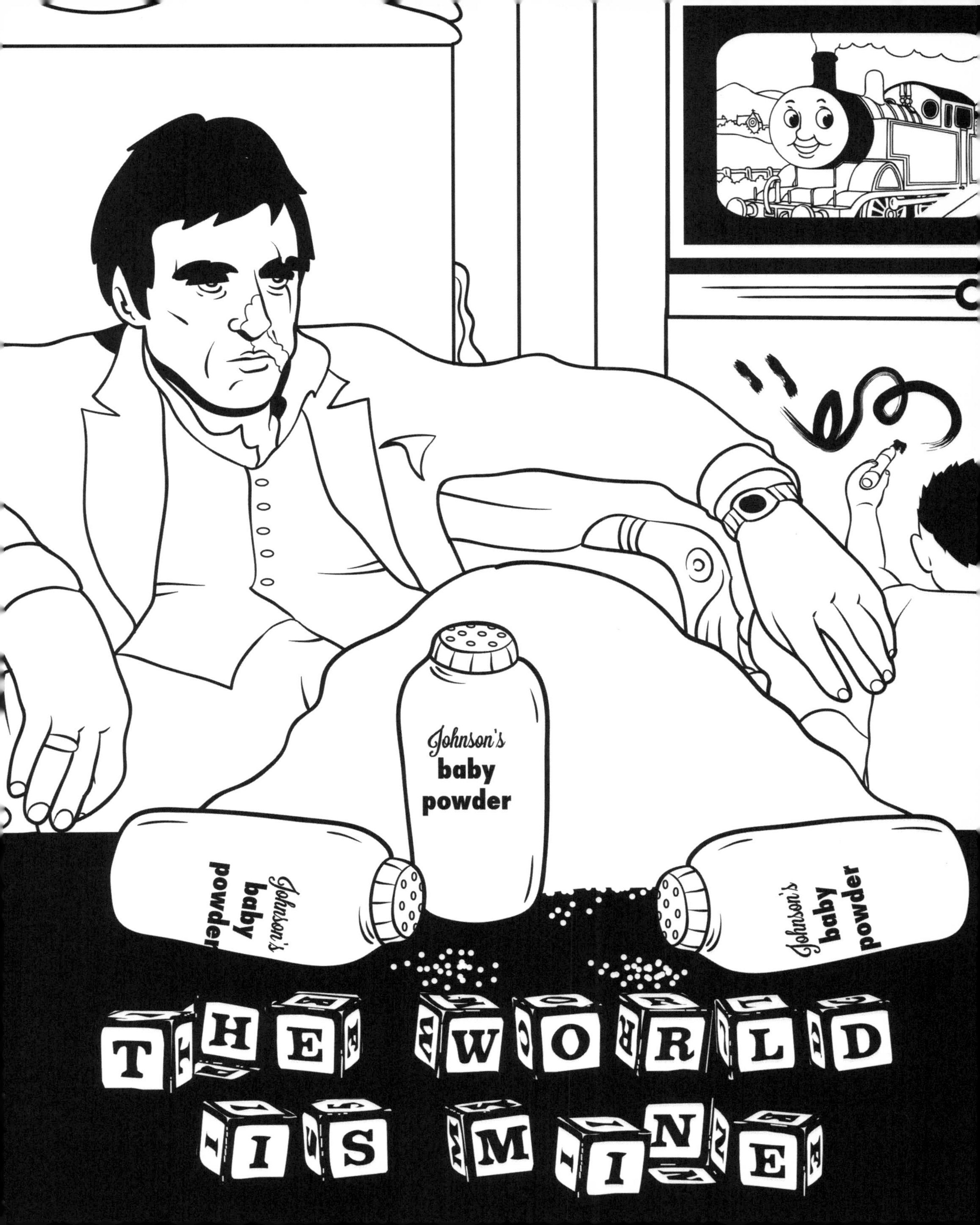
Johnson's baby powder
Johnson's baby powder
Johnson's baby powder
THE WORLD
IS MINE

EPILOGUE

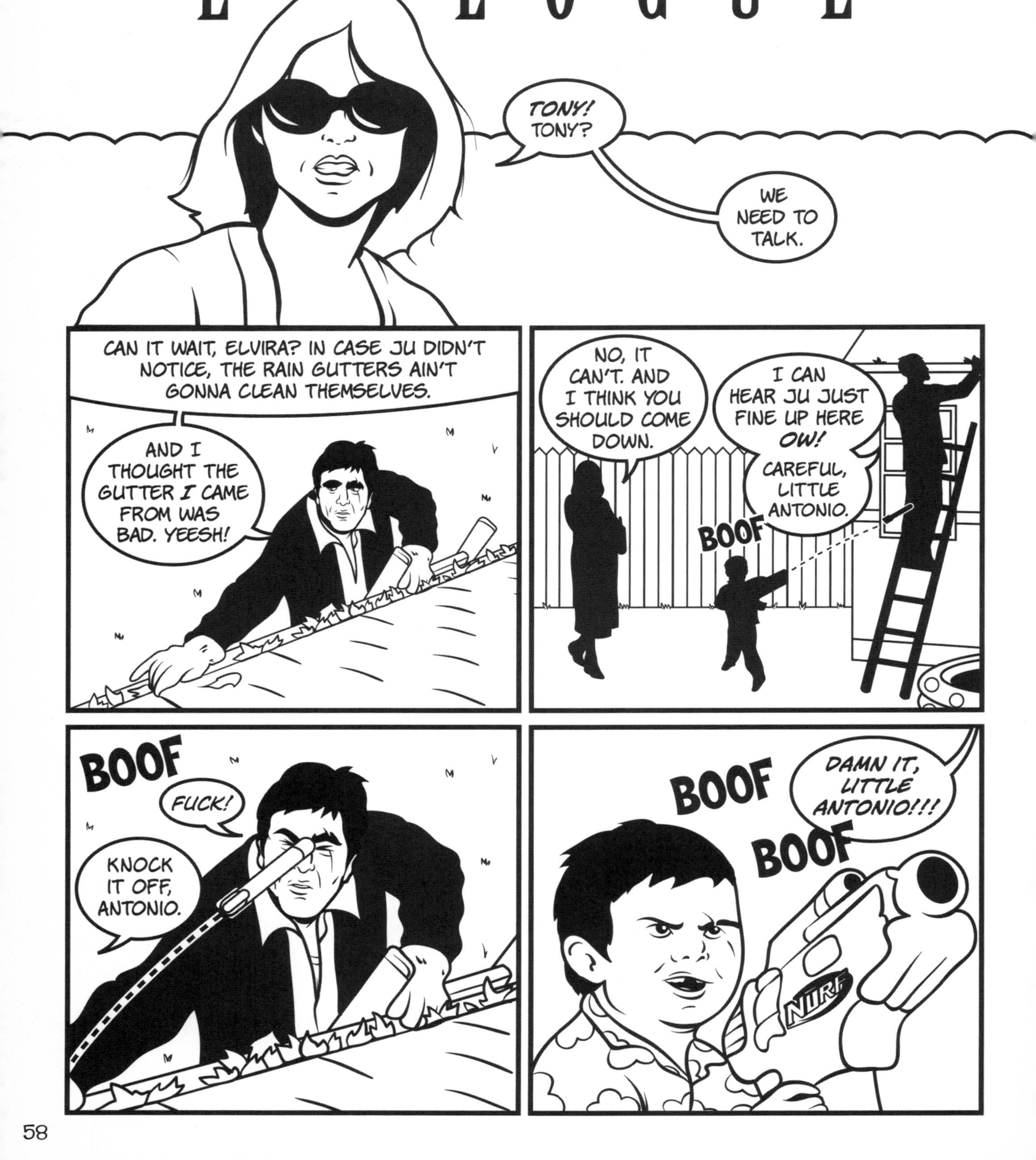
TONY! TONY?
WE NEED TO TALK.
CAN IT WAIT, ELVIRA? IN CASE JU DIDN'T NOTICE, THE RAIN GUTTERS AIN'T GONNA CLEAN THEMSELVES.
AND I THOUGHT THE GUTTER I CAME FROM WAS BAD. YEESH!
NO, IT CAN'T. AND I THINK YOU SHOULD COME DOWN.
I CAN HEAR JU JUST FINE UP HERE OW!
BOOF
CAREFUL, LITTLE ANTONIO.
BOOF
FUCK!
KNOCK IT OFF, ANTONIO.
BOOF
DAMN IT, LITTLE ANTONIO!!!
BOOF
NERF

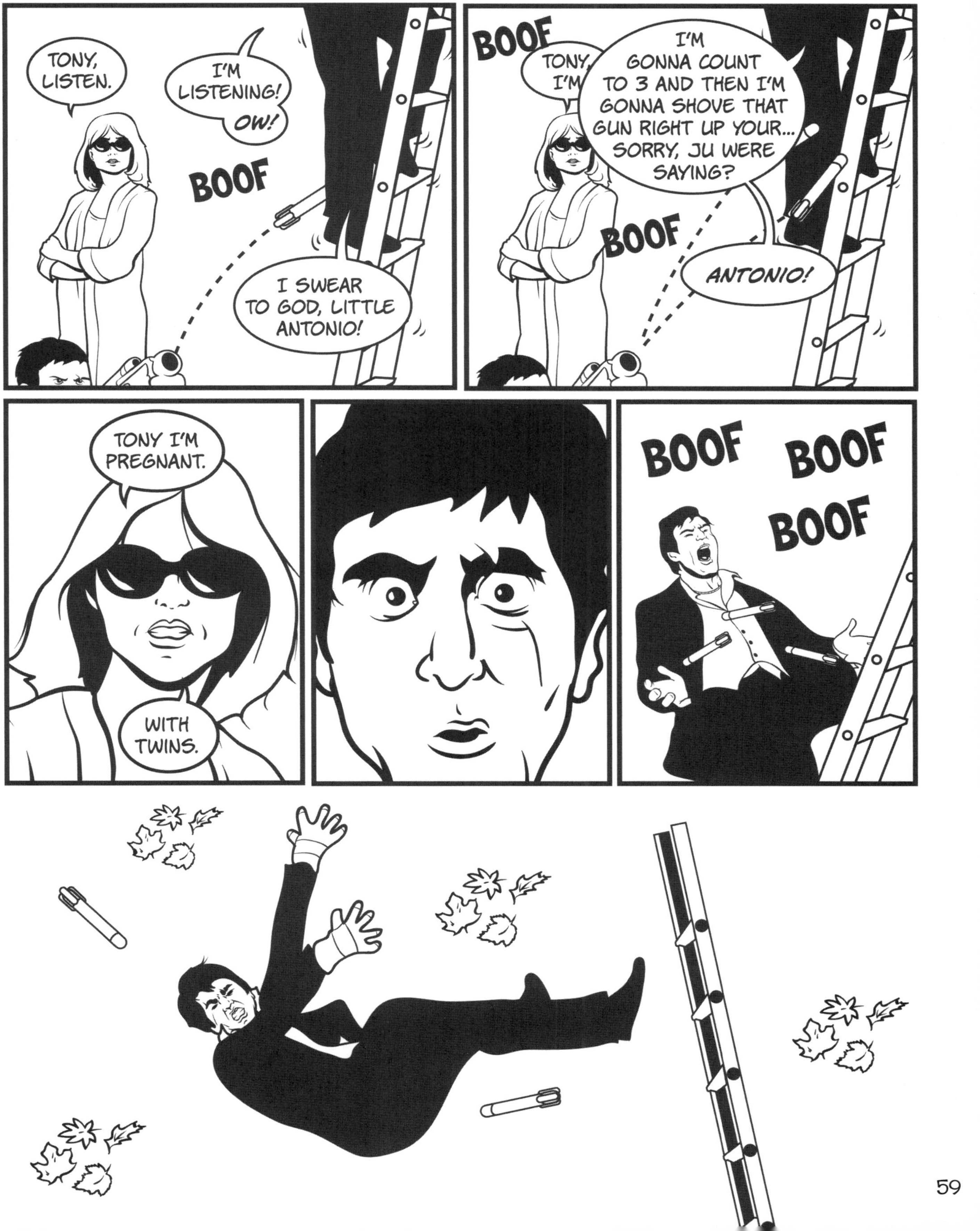
TONY, LISTEN.
I'M LISTENING!
OW!
BOOF
I SWEAR TO GOD, LITTLE ANTONIO!
BOOF
TONY, I'M
I'M GONNA COUNT TO 3 AND THEN I'M GONNA SHOVE THAT GUN RIGHT UP YOUR... SORRY, JU WERE SAYING?
BOOF
ANTONIO!
TONY I'M PREGNANT.
WITH TWINS.
BOOF
BOOF
BOOF

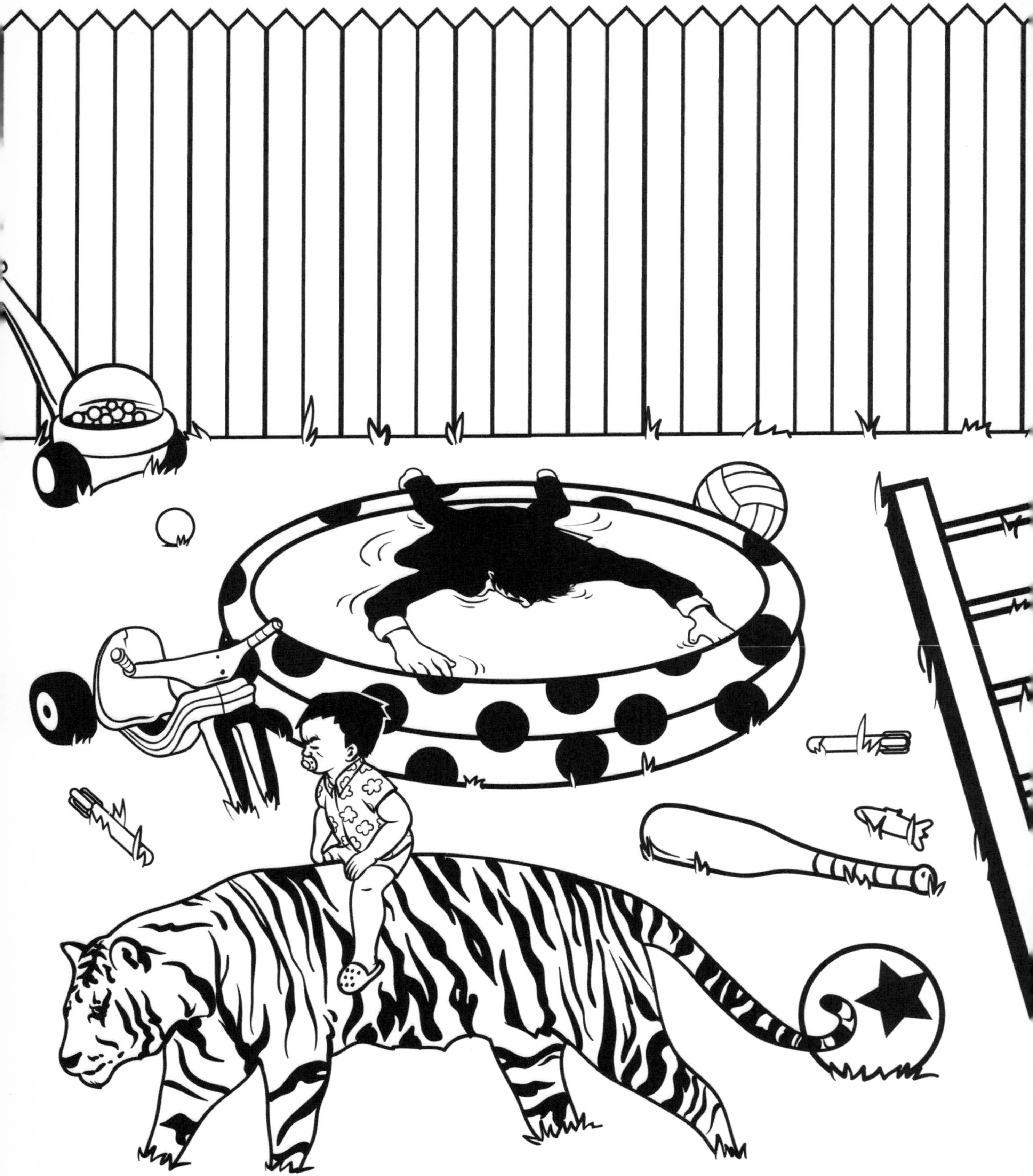

Name: _____   Date: _____

"POP" QUIZ

1. What kind of pet does Tony have?
_____
- -
_____

2. What does Tony name his baby?
_____
- -
_____

3. Who does Tony trust?
_____
- -
_____

4. How many teaspoons of sugar are in a kilo? Show your work!
_____
- -
_____

5. What is Tony's least favorite book?
_____
- -
_____

6. How does Tony get his kid into the fancy daycare?
_____
- -
_____

7. What does Tony dress as for Halloween?
_____
- -
_____

 **Did you find all the Goodyear Blimps hidden in this book?**

JU DID IT!

Congratulations on surviving my activity book. Looks like ju got what it takes to survive parenthood after all.

Welcome to the gang.

Proud Member of the
STAY AT HOME
SCARFACE
Parenting Cartel

_____
Signature

WHO PUT THIS THING TOGETHER?
FILL IN THE BLANKS TO CREATE YOUR OWN AUTHOR BIO!

Kenny Keil is a _writer_ and _artist_.
Your Name — Thing you're pretty good at — Thing you're OK at

His work has appeared in _MAD Magazine_, _Vibe Magazine_, and
Humor Magazine — Music Magazine

The Devastator. His other works are _Rhyme Travelers_, _Death Trip_
Some Other Thing — All-Ages Comic — Sci-Fi Comic

and _Tales to Suffice_. He's also a _stay at home dad_
Humor Comic — What you do all day

and a _gangster movie enthusiast_. He lives in _the Los Angeles area_
What you really do all day — Location (be vague)

with his _wife & son_ and _0_ cats. _Kenny_ has
Family Members — # of cats — Your name again

received numerous awards, including _a spelling bee trophy in 2nd grade_.
Most prestigious award you've ever received